W9-DAU-635

May Paomay Tung, PhD

Chinese Americans and Their Immigrant Parents
Conflict, Identity, and Values

More pre-publication
REVIEWS, COMMENTARIES, EVALUATIONS . . .

"Like good soup, this book nourishes on more than one level. Rich with information, but also with qualities of the heart, it is a treasure-house of information on Chinese and Chinese-American personalities; differences between Chinese, Chinese-American, and European-American emotional styles and family structures; and the impact of past and current waves of immigration on the Chinese-American experience. It succinctly conveys a career's lessons on psychotherapy with Chinese immigrants and Chinese Americans. However, like all good books, it goes beyond itself. All clinicians interested in cross-cultural themes, and anyone interested in the Asian-American encounter, will find that this book provokes fruitful reflection on questions of self, identity, culture, cross-cultural dilemmas and the path toward their solution, family, psychotherapy, and much more. There is real wisdom here, and it is communicated with grace and a delightfully engaging style."

Richard Ruth, PhD
Medical Staff,
CPC Health/Chestnut
Lodge Hospital;
Faculty, Washington
School of Psychiatry

"Tung brings to this book her experience working with Chinese Americans and their immigrant parents in her practice as well as her own personal background. She has defined and elaborated upon an approach to dealing with 'differences' within a family, which are nonetheless frequently culture- and values-based. As is the case in any cross-cultural encounter, the more each participant knows of the other's culturally derived values, the better the chance for understanding and respect to be built. In the case of this book, the view is of two related but distinctly different generations of Chinese that give the reader insight not only into that specific context, but also into the much broader world of cross-cultural differences in general.

I would recommend this book to any therapist working with multiple generations within a family; to any teacher or professor teaching psychology, intercultural communication, Asian studies, and many other disciplines; and to general readers interested in how cultures and the values we acquire within them affect our relationships."

Toby S. Frank
President,
Intercultural Press,
Yarmouth, ME

The Haworth Clinical Practice Press
An Imprint of The Haworth Press, Inc.
New York • London • Oxford

Chinese Americans
and Their Immigrant Parents
Conflict, Identity, and Values

HAWORTH Marriage and the Family
Terry S. Trepper, PhD
Executive Editor

Adolescents and Their Families: An Introduction to Assessment and Intervention by Mark Worden

Parents Whose Parents Were Divorced by R. Thomas Berner

The Effect of Children on Parents by Anne-Marie Ambert

Multigenerational Family Therapy by David S. Freeman

Therapy with Treatment Resistant Families: A Consultation-Crisis Intervention Model by William George McCown, Judith Johnson, and Associates

Developing Healthy Stepfamilies: Twenty Families Tell Their Stories by Patricia Kelley

Propagations: Thirty Years of Influence from the Mental Research Institute edited by John H. Weakland and Wendel A. Ray

Structured Exercises for Promoting Family and Group Strengths: A Handbook for Group Leaders, Trainers, Educators, Counselors, and Therapists edited by Ron McManus and Glen Jennings

Making Families Work and What to Do When They Don't: Thirty Guides for Imperfect Parents of Imperfect Children by Bill Borcherdt

Family Therapy of Neurobehavioral Disorders: Integrating Neuropsychology and Family Therapy by Judith Johnson and William McCown

Parents, Children, and Adolescents: Interactive Relationships and Development in Context by Anne-Marie Ambert

Women Survivors of Childhood Sexual Abuse: Healing Through Group Work: Beyond Survival by Judy Chew

Tales from Family Therapy: Life-Changing Clinical Experiences edited by Frank N. Thomas and Thorana S. Nelson

The Therapist's Notebook: Homework, Handouts, and Activities for Use in Psychotherapy edited by Lorna L. Hecker and Sharon A. Deacon

The Web of Poverty: Psychosocial Perspectives by Anne-Marie Ambert

Stepfamilies: A Multi-Dimensional Perspective by Roni Berger

Clinical Applications of Bowen Family Systems Theory by Peter Titelman

Treating Children in Out-of-Home Placements by Marvin Rosen

Your Family, Inc.: Practical Tips for Building a Healthy Family Business by Ellen Frankenberg

Therapeutic Intervention with Poor, Unorganized Families: From Distress to Hope by Shlomo A. Sharlin and Michal Shamai

The Residential Youth Care Worker in Action: A Collaborative, Competency-Based Approach by Robert Bertolino and Kevin Thompson

Chinese Americans and Their Immigrant Parents: Conflict, Identity, and Values by May Paomay Tung

Together Through Thick and Thin: A Multinational Picture of Long-Term Marriages by Shlomo A. Sharlin, Florence W. Kaslow, and Helga Hammerschmidt

Chinese Americans
and Their Immigrant Parents
Conflict, Identity, and Values

May Paomay Tung, PhD

The Haworth Clinical Practice Press
An Imprint of The Haworth Press, Inc.
New York • London • Oxford

4286/888

Published by

The Haworth Clinical Practice Press, Inc., an imprint of The Haworth Press, Inc., 10 Alice Street, Binghamton, NY 13904-1580

Cover design by Marylouise E. Doyle.

Library of Congress Cataloging-in-Publication Data

Tung, May Pao-may.
    Chinese Americans and their immigrant parents : conflict, identity, and values / May Paomay Tung.
        p.   cm.
    Includes bibliographical references and index.
    ISBN 0-7890-1055-0 (alk. paper)—ISBN 0-7890-1056-9 (pbk. : alk. paper)
    1. Chinese Americans—Ethnic identity. 2. Chinese Americans—Family relationships. 3. Chinese Americans—Psychology. 4. Chinese American families. 5. Immigrants—Family relationships. 6. Parent and adult child—United States. I. Title.

E184.C5 T85 2000
305.8951073—dc21
                                                                                99-056008

To the Memories of My Parents

董 朱 嶷
Mrs. Tung Chu Nei

董 时 进
Dr. Tung Shih-Tsin

In
Gratitude

ABOUT THE AUTHOR

May Tung, PhD, is a clinical psychologist in private practice in San Francisco, California. She is the former Director of the National Asian American Psychology Training Center in San Francisco. The author of several journal articles about cross-cultural psychology, Dr. Tung is also a contributing editor to the *American Journal of Orthopsychiatry.* She speaks Mandarin Chinese and Shanghai and Sichuan dialects and has served as a consultant and lecturer in China.

CONTENTS

Acknowledgments

This book has many "inhabitants" who breathed life into the pages. My gratitude goes first to the young Chinese-American professionals who worked with me in their personal psychotherapy: You know who you are. Through you I would like to thank your parents; they tried their best to hold up the sky so that you may have a chance and that I may meet you.

The following colleagues, friends, and family members have all read the manuscript at different stages: Tom Banks, May Koo Chu, E. E. Ho, Vera Tung Preston, Zelda Porte, and Kathy Tung. For your encouragement, comments, and valuable time, I would like to thank you. You made working on this project easier for me. A touch of family sentiment goes to Hubert, Laura, and their children, Andi and Anming, for "opening" this book for me. The rest of the family will be next!

Separate recognition goes to my dear friend Catherine Davis. Cathy voluntarily edited the very "raw" first draft—a sign of her friendship and courage! She also served as my "lay reader at large." She gave me many insights and suggestions, showing her keen mind and wealth of knowledge. I am deeply in debt to her patience and good humor.

Introduction

This book is organically grown. It simply grew out of my life as a Chinese-American clinical psychologist doing psychotherapy, training, reading, thinking, observing, and introspecting. For a long time these activities were carried out without any conscious unifying cultural frame of reference. To take one's cultural background into consideration in psychotherapy is a recent development, still in its infancy. It was simply not part of psychology's consciousness in the earlier years when I was in school and in training.

The portion of my clinical work responsible for this book is conducting psychotherapy with young Chinese-American professionals. It was a gradual and almost imperceptible process that eventually formed the focus of my practice. As I listened to them with an unbiased, naive mind, I began to detect, aside from their personal and familial circumstances, common themes in their difficulties that, I concluded, related to their shared Chinese background. These themes, in relation to their families, include a sense of parental disapproval or emotional withholding ("It's never good enough"), inadequate or mistaken guidance, role reversals, and puzzling beliefs and behaviors. In relation to society at large, they often feel unsure of themselves, not knowing who they are. The sense of being "invisible" or overlooked is pervasive. I began to see that much of the intergenerational and societal conflicts basically stems from intercultural misunderstandings and antagonism. Our society and the world, as a matter of fact, seem to have an abundance of both.

Even though these difficult Chinese-American personal situations were the original inspiration, this book is not about psychotherapy with, or psychopathology of, this population. Instead, I will try to relate and connect the immediate problems and conditions to their sources in Chinese and American cultures and histories, as well as in the immigration experience. Behavior is largely learned. It is shaped by familial, social, and cultural influences. The same behavior may be appropriate in China but not in the United States, and vice versa. To know the origin and meaning of a behavior may help us to be less judgmental and more appreciative. Toward this end, I will contrast differing concepts in personal boundary, values and beliefs, ways of expressing emotions, and styles in problem solving. Colloquial language and everyday behavior are cited to illustrate the complexity in the region where East meets West. It is in this region where the young must live and the elders must raise their children. It is here where Chinese-American self-identity and integration take place. No personal "case histories" will be used in this book.

There are a few inherent difficulties in writing a book of this nature. First, to write about the interactions of individual lives and their cultural background is like trying to find a beginning and an end of a sphere: There is none. All parts are interrelated. Life is not linear. Therefore, in this book, the same behaviors or issues can be discussed in more than one context. Second, cultural differences, when looked at out of context, may appear to be only a matter of degree. An analogy is that different paintings may use similar colors and lines but each painting is unmistakenly "itself." It is, therefore, in the total gestalt that we find the uniqueness of each culture. Finally, in presenting Chinese-American experiences, I am not at all saying that the Chinese "had it worst." I see no value in comparing who "suffered" the most. Yet, such comparisons are often the reactions of audiences when one or the other group is being discussed.

This book, of course, does not pretend to be "comprehensive." My hope is to highlight some of the psychocultural dynamics underlying our behavior in order to "translate," to make sense of, the differences. Terms such as "white," "Caucasian," "West," and "mainstream" are used in a colloquial sense for easier reading. Even though the book is intended for the general public, I believe it is also appropriate for mental health professionals, educators, and anyone engaged in intercultural work with the Chinese and with Chinese Americans. I further hope that this slim volume will cause a momentary pause for journalists and politicians, "Hmm, I didn't know that," before making their pronouncements.

Chapter 1

What Is in a Name?
Culture and Personal Boundary

When my oldest nephew and his wife, who is Caucasian, were expecting their second child, a Chinese name was given by the grandfather, my oldest brother. The expectant mother asked me about the wording of the Chinese name, as they planned to use it as the child's middle name on her birth certificate.

"How should we word her Chinese name?"

"Anming."

"But 'An' is also her brother Andi's name."

"Yes. The two words go together; 'An' is their generational name."

"What is hers and hers alone?"

"Ming."

"How will people call her by her Chinese name?"

"Anming."

"What is her complete Chinese name?"

"Tung Anming."

This exchange once again reminded me of the vast cultural differences in personal boundary and their implications. By "boundary," in this context, I refer to a sense of knowing where one stops and others begin, the proper degree of concern for other persons, and the source of energy and motivation in life decisions. There are countless ways to address this all-pervasive phenomenon. Clarity about boundaries is important because it is the basis for self-identity, social and interpersonal interactions, and belief and value systems. There are implications in practically everything we do or do not do. I chose three areas to demonstrate these implications because they are among the most familiar aspects of daily living, namely, one's name, the individual person's role in society and in marriage, and the ways in which our dwellings reflect boundary issues of who are the insiders and who are the outsiders.

WHAT IS IN A CHINESE NAME?

If we think of a Chinese person as more like a branch of a tree or a musician in a symphony orchestra and not as a separate tree or a soloist, we may be able to better understand what is symbolized in her or his name.

Unlike in the West, Chinese always place the family name first, then the "generational" name, and last, one's individual given name. In some cases, the generational name may come last, with some people having only two words to their names. Even in these cases there is usually a family theme, such as all names are precious stones, large evergreen trees, mythical animals, or words reflecting traditional Chinese values. Chinese names are almost always chosen because of some meaning that the family wishes to represent or express. One is not named after someone. That is considered being disrespectful, and it also means cutting short the "longevity," even after death, of the person for whom one is named. In spirit one "lives" forever, which is consistent with Chinese ancestor worship tradition.

The most intriguing part to me is the generational name. In our example, "An" means peace, tranquility, or security. This word appears in the names of all children who share the same grandfather, great-grandfather, and beyond on the father's side of the family. By seeing the family name and the generational name one can immediately place oneself in the proper lineage "slot," knowing how one is related to the others. The effect can be magical, at least it was for me. When I first met my uncle's children in China, pieces of a large puzzle fell into place at high-tech speed! This brought an immediate sense of belonging and closeness, a feeling that much can be taken for granted because we already "know" something about one another. After all, two out of the three words in all of our names are the same.

One way of detecting cultural values is to study the degree of linguistic refinement regarding certain aspects of life. For example, the English word "cousin" is all-inclusive. In Chinese, different terms specify generation, gender, paternal or maternal side, and birth order to indicate precisely how two persons are related. Using this familial "blueprint" as a basis, relational terms are also generously applied to other non-blood-related persons to show goodwill and to pull for closer ties. My siblings and I addressed our parents' contemporaries as "aunts" and "uncles" long into our adulthood. These terms of address are even more endearing when one is away from home, as expressed in the Chinese saying

在家靠父母在外靠 朋友
zaijia   kao   fumu, zaiwai   kao   pengyou

When at home, one depends on one's parents.
When away from home, one depends on friends.

The word *kao* literally means "to lean on," showing the interdependent nature of Chinese relationships. The persons one can count on the most are one's family members. To address non-blood-related persons with familial titles is both to honor them

---

Calligraphy of Chinese characters throughout the book by Meng-so Tsia-Pollar, PhD.

and to establish mutual support. Such mutuality is especially essential when one is overseas in a hostile environment, as was the case in most of the family origins of Chinese Americans. To cluster together for protection is not only a tradition but a necessity, even to this day.

As with practically everything in life, there are always two sides to a coin. When cultural values and traditions are carried to an extreme and demanded indiscriminately, the results will be problematic. This is true no matter in which culture or what values. Chinese family emphasis can be a source of support, an anchor and a haven, but it can also be suffocating and paralyzing. If I were to name one particular area of life in which the Chinese Americans I see in psychotherapy have the most problems, it would be the area of family of origin. Most other problems are derivatives. This may sound shocking, but the phenomenon is actually quite universal. In the days of ancient Greek tragedies, the power of family feud in the form of intrafamily intrigue and murder was portrayed. Freud made famous the drama of Oedipus who killed his father and married his mother as foretold by an oracle at his birth.

A "birth oracle" symbolizes the innate, inevitable nature of familial complications that no one can escape completely. Differences are found in the role and value assigned to "family" and how each culture resolves conflicts. In an individualistic culture the young are expected to go off and be a separate "tree." Even in this arrangement, psychodynamically oriented psychotherapists know well how much time and energy is devoted to "transference." This term means, basically, one's perceptions of others may be distorted based on one's experiences with one's parents. In Chinese and Chinese-American cases, the saliency lies in dealing with the conflicts while the parties live in close proximity, both in physical distance and frequency of contact (Tung, 1991). I have been repeatedly amazed by the amount of mutual assistance that exists when the chips are down, no matter how excruciating the conflicts, in the Chinese-American families I know. In China and in the immigrant parents' generation, even friends receive such painstaking personal support. Often, requests and expectations do not need to be expressed to be met. People simply know what to do, for example, when there is illness, death, or birth. Inconveniences to oneself are overlooked. We have to keep in mind, however, that these actions must be mutual and continuous to work smoothly and to avoid a strong sense of social wrongdoing.

The American counterpart for such "comprehensive coverage" is the extensive variety of insurances we buy, the support groups, sororities and fraternities, professional and civic organizations, etc. The basic difference is that a Chinese person is born into a group while the American person joins by choice. The former is permanent, the latter, usually temporary. There are advantages and shortcomings in both cases. In the Chinese-American families I know, mutual assistance is often provided in times of financial and medical difficulties. Parents and children buying homes for each other is a common practice. The helping hand is also automatically extended to other blood relatives, such as bringing them to the United States, a practice responsible to a large degree for the increased Chinese population in this country.

The reliability and effectiveness of such traditional mutual assistance, interestingly, was demonstrated in San Francisco's Chinatown during the Great Depression. While some Chinese men lost their jobs along with the rest of the country's workers, Chinese-American women, who mostly worked within the Chinese community, were able to maintain their jobs, improve their circumstances, and keep their families together. Second, since very few Chinese invested in stocks and bonds, owned property, or had savings accounts because of their low-paying jobs, they were less affected by the economic disaster. Third, the "town fathers" put their energy into procuring whatever resources were available from China as well as ensuring that their people were not denied public assistance to which they were entitled in this country (Yung, 1995).

In reading this book, it should be remembered that this all-pervasive tradition of mutual assistance did work for the Chinese, at home and abroad, and this is the continuing expectation Chinese immigrant parents have of their children. Parents enforce methods that worked for them. They are not "bad" parents. The younger generation, however, is caught between a past that is puzzling to them and a present they cannot live up to, be it Chinese or American style.

INDIVIDUAL PERSONS IN CHINESE CONTEXT

The Self

Most of the young Chinese-American professionals in psychotherapy with me have used the word "confusion": where does oneself end and others begin? "I always put other people's feelings first. I don't even know how *I* feel." "Is it selfish/bad/wrong to think of oneself first?" Moving out of the parental home before one is married is looked upon as being selfish; visits less than once a week displease the parents; not living up to parental expectations is frowned upon. And, there are the relatives who want to know and comment on how *xiayidai,* the younger generation, is doing, to the pride or chagrin of the parents. It is true, East or West, that children are reflections of their parents. In Chinese tradition, the children are more part of the parents, not mere reflections. The valued overlapping personal boundary is sometimes compounded by poverty and large families, so that many Chinese Americans grow up in physically cramped spaces as well.

In recent years, I have seen a few persons who are new emigrants from China. I noticed the large casts of characters when they tried to tell me about their situations and how these circumstances evolved. Relatives, co-workers, supervisors, neighbors, and, in one case, the landlady of a cousin living in Canada—all had a hand in one another's lives. At the same time, they also offer endless accounts of mutual assistance, as described earlier, and discuss how just the thought of family sustained them through their ordeals during political upheavals, such as the infamous Cultural Revolution. These Chinese are referring to *zijiren,* literally, "self-person," meaning all those who are close and important to one's life and history.

A few years ago I saw an interracial couple. The Caucasian husband spoke no Chinese, and the Chinese wife spoke little English. The husband requested that I ask his wife if she was willing to make a commitment to their marriage: "We've gone around this over and over again, looking [it] up in the dictionary, getting nowhere." My immediate reaction was, how do you say "commitment" in Chinese? I then proceeded to explain to the wife what Americans mean by that word in the context of a marriage. A few sentences into my explanation she waved her hand to show how useless it all was: "We Chinese, we are married; we are married." What she meant was that it is not up to the individual whether to make the "commitment" or not. Once one is married, one is married for good. That evening I looked in my English-Chinese dictionary. "Commitment" is only cited in connection with business dealings, such as a contract. It is not an issue in personal matters. To make a commitment implies two separate independent parties have free choices. This phenomenon of overlapping boundary finds an eloquent enactment in formal Chinese banquets. There, one is not supposed to help oneself to the food. Instead, both the host and all the guests heap food on one another's plates. Everyone is amply fed at the end, without anyone ever having served oneself, a true symbol of interdependence. All for one and one for all seems an appropriate motto.

The pervasive "other-aware" (in contrast to "self-aware") interconnectedness seems to me to be the basic reason why so few Chinese Americans or Chinese societies can relate to Western-style dynamic psychotherapy; in therapy one has to step out of the familiar to be a stranger and look into oneself. While in the West the "self" is "consistently connected to the attainment of a degree of reflective awareness" (Johnson, 1985, p. 94), the Chinese "self," as Hsu (1971) delineated, penetrates all the way into and through layers of interrelatedness with other persons, societies, and the "spiritual" world, as indicated by Chinese beliefs in "fate," "destiny," and ancestors. To this, Chinese Americans must also add their immigration history and adjustment. Effective psychotherapy has to include all these layers and spheres of meanings, a fiercely challenging demand for Western-trained psychotherapists. Personal boundary is also closely related to problem-solving styles and the role of emotions, which will be the themes of Chapter 4. Going outside of one's personal world to an "irrelevant" stranger is simply not the Chinese idea of an effective way to solve problems.

In addition, the inward-connected tendency of the Chinese and the outward-moving position of Westerners can be expected to clash in intercultural comparisons. To use a recent example, during the 1998 Winter Olympics, Michelle Kwan, a Chinese-American skater, and Tara Lipinski, a Caucasian American, were compared: "Lipinski and Kwan stuck to completely different schedules at Nagano," reports *Time* magazine (Labi, 1998, pp. 67-68). "Journalists handicapped the event in favor of Lipinski because she was so carefree and relaxed. She was all over the Olympic village. . . . Kwan, in contrast . . . [i]nstead of sharing cramped quarters with Lipinski and the flu that took Germany's skater Tanja Szewczenko out of the running, bunked with Mom and Dad at a hotel (Its location was kept secret)." "Mom and Dad" infantilizes a person more than the word "parents." Earlier in the same report, referring to Lipinski who was fifteen (Kwan was seventeen), "On Friday . . . in her parents' hotel room, the 15-year-old just wanted her mother's comfort. 'It's O.K. to be scared. It's good to be scared.' said Pat Lipinski. 'But you can do it.'" Here, the scene between child and parent is portrayed at a much more mature level, with attention paid to feelings. The report continues: "Conventional wisdom says Kwan should have played it differently, a little looser perhaps" (Labi, 1998, pp. 67-68). I also watched the interview when both skaters were present. The interviewer brought up Kwan's living arrangement again. It is as though Kwan had to justify herself for staying with "Mom and Dad." This type of inquisition and curiosity, in effect, is saying, "What you are doing is strange and wrong," a message Chinese Americans receive only too frequently. I have known both Asian and non-Asian mental health workers trained in America who, in treating Asians living with their parents, would automatically consider such an arrangement pathological and make it a treatment goal that the person should move out and live independently.

The ultimate symbol for Chinese interdependence is inherent in the word *ren,* the highest virtue in the Chinese value system. The word is formed with a "human" root and the number "two," 仁, and is therefore interpersonal in nature. This word, not surprisingly, has no English equivalent. It embraces qualities of love in a broad and humanistic sense, benevolence, compassion, and respect for others. The word is so fundamental to the Chinese that it is depicted on numerous decorative household articles to serve as a constant reminder.

It may be illuminating at this juncture to take a look at the often-debated issue of "human rights." Simply stated, human rights is an individualistic concept and value. A person need only be born to be entitled to these "rights." To the Chinese mind, if the conflict is between one individual and an entire group, the former clearly carries less weight. The Chinese individual must earn her or his place in society by serving and by being valuable to other persons. The Chinese individual, in other words, is never evaluated in isolation or in absolute terms. One's "entitlement" is always considered in the context of how one fits into the larger goal.

Let me give an example. In a Chinese language newspaper, I noticed an item that illustrates this East-West difference. Shi Cheng, a town in Jiang Xi Province (central China), holds elections of city officials. In the past few years, a total of forty-two persons were not reelected because, in the residents' evaluations, they were considered not "filial": they did not treat their parents well (*New Continent*, 1997). Even in a Western-style "democratic" practice, the Chinese are, first of all, family oriented. Family, as we know by now, is the basis for group-oriented philosophy in life. In Chinese thinking, the suffering of a reference group, such as one's family or village, is by far more serious than individual suffering.

Liang Qichao, a journalist recognized as China's foremost modern intellectual, visited the United States in 1903. While observing American democracy and Chinese character he wrote, "Our (Chinese) character is that of clansmen rather than citizens" (Liang, 1903, p. 92). Clansmen relate to local community concerns and citizens, national concerns. American-style democracy requires citizens. After nearly a century this shrewd observation still seems true, and it is directly related to the Chinese sense of personal boundary.

In China's legal system today, for example, adult children are held responsible for elderly parents who are without a pension or other means of livelihood. For Western societies to expect China to observe "human rights" and democracy in an individualistic sense would be as arbitrary and futile as if China were to base its foreign and trade policies on Western countries' level of filial piety! However, in the new fluidity of the world today, I believe it will be beneficial to continue the dialogue on the history, development, and relative benefits of each position. The value of such an exchange, I felt, was illustrated as I watched PBS News-Hour on May 22, 1998. I noted a pairing of the extremes. The NewsHour had a feature on the Springfield, Oregon, killing involving a fifteen-year-old boy who shot and killed his parents and two schoolmates and wounded a number of others in the school cafeteria. The other feature story was on Indonesia's student revolt and Suharto's resignation after days of bloodshed and chaos. Here, we have the pairing of an authoritarian, dictatorial, Asian patriarchal system and a narcissistic, impulse-ridden American acting out. Both are excessive, dysfunctional, and diseased. Strange how opposites meet at the end when carried to extremes. Eastern and Western people can learn a great deal from one another.

Returning to the Chinese-American "self" and adjustment in an individualistic culture, I often hear self-criticisms from Chinese Americans and their wishes to be more "assertive" and "confrontational" in their dealings with their parents and people in general. Being confrontational, assertive, rebellious, and stressing the negative are all ways a person can differentiate oneself from others en route to individualism. During the 1995 United Nations' Women's Conference in Beijing, China, I noticed how the American media consistently reported on the conflicts and discord. Chinese Central Television, on the other hand, reported how well everybody got along. If one did not know they were reporting on the same event, one would not have guessed it from the contents of their reports! By stressing conflicts, the American reporters highlighted the differences among the groups and made each stand out separately. By emphasizing the commonalties, the Chinese media painted a harmonious picture of the world, enclosed in one single image. Chinese tend to deal with conflicts in private. Many young Chinese Americans, however, feel they should also challenge and "do something" about their differences with their parents, in keeping with what they see all around them.

They want to separate themselves from the original "tree"; they want to change the boundary.

The Self in Marriage

In the popular film from Taiwan, *Wedding Banquet,* a Chinese-American son went through a great deal of trouble to hide the fact that he was gay when his parents were about to come for a visit. The disguise was so airtight that he actually fathered a son in a "cover-up" marriage. At that point, his father calmly acknowledged that he had known all along that his son is a homosexual. He went along with the "game" just to get a grandson. He achieved his goal. To continue the family line is much more important to the father than his son's sexual preference. I have had homosexual Chinese Americans in psychotherapy with me. Their situations can be excruciatingly difficult, with nothing movie-worthy or comical about most of them. Even interracial marriages can be a reason for profound apprehension and tactful handling. A marriage with an "outsider" means breaking away from the core. In therapy sessions, much time is devoted to trying to understand the parents personally and culturally and to forming "strategies" accordingly. It would be a mistake for the children to confront the parents, to put them on the spot. Confrontation requires stark individuality. To maintain their dignity or to save face, the parents would then have to stand their ground. This is not to "trick" "old-fashioned" parents. It is a matter of how to soften the boundary to allow an opportunity for changes to take place. As in an organ transplant, alien organs have to be compatible with the entire body to be accepted.

To the Chinese, marriages are not simply one's "own business," but a matter of continuation of family blood and name. I cannot recall a single case among the young Chinese Americans I have treated when the question of marriage was not presented and considered to some degree, within the family frame of reference. Some of them may not even have noticed that they did this.

Many of them actually introduced the topic with words spoken by family members and friends, even though the comments may be recalled with annoyance. The pressure for an adult daughter or son to marry far exceeds any such pressure in Western families of today. To the Chinese, perhaps less true for Chinese Americans, marriage is more a pragmatic, though personally important, milestone in life, a responsibility rather than individualistic romanticism.

In "International Preferences in Selecting Mates" (Buss et al., 1990), researchers used 9,474 individuals from thirty-three countries on six continents. The average age of the participants was twenty-three. Of the participants, 500 were from China and 566 from Taiwan, making a total of 1,066 ethnic Chinese in the study and 1,491 subjects from mainland United States. These are the two largest sample groups, and also the two in which we are most interested. Research subjects were requested to rank eighteen characteristics on desirability in a mate. Results were grouped into a "traditional" and a "modern" orientation toward mating:

> [T]he former placing great value on chastity, home and children, domestic skills and resource provisioning and the latter devaluating these traditional attributes. (p. 45)

As a whole, we can say the China sample, especially the men, seems to be more "traditional," practical, and family oriented. The one interesting item is "chastity," defined as "No previous experiences in sexual intercourse." Male China subjects ranked chastity number three in valued attributes for their future wives. This same item was ranked second from the last by American men and as the least important by American women subjects. China and Taiwan female subjects assigned a medium importance to this item. On the other end of the spectrum, what we may consider as more "modern" and individualistic, "mutual attraction," is valued by Taiwan and U.S. subjects but less so by the China samples. The men in the China sample ranked it number four and the women, number eight. The item "emotional stability and maturity" is a priority for all, but less so for China male subjects, who ranked it number five. In this item we see a desire for a long-lasting personal quality that is necessary for an enduring relationship. The fact that the China male sample did not place as high a priority on it, I think, may be related to what we discussed earlier; namely, marital commitment is not as much of a choice in China, and, therefore, "long lasting" is more "guaranteed." Interestingly enough, "good looks" only received a middle to clearly unimportant ranking from the entire international sample. Even in the U.S. sample, male subjects ranked it number seven and females, number thirteen.

In reviewing the previous data we should remember how life circumstances influence one's outlook on life events. That more similarities exist between Taiwan and U.S. groups than between China and Taiwan groups may largely be due to the fact that China has had much less exposure to Western lifestyle than Taiwan and the questionnaire originated in the United States. Conspicuous in their absence, for example, are items eliciting family acceptability of the future mate or questions about filial qualities. Would we then have greater differences between the Taiwan and U.S. samples and more similarities between the Taiwan and China samples? As a matter of fact, the very omission of culturally relevant items illustrates precisely the difficulties of Chinese Americans in their negotiation in American lifestyle. I have seen Chinese-American individuals and couples for whom the lack of family acceptability became a serious problem in their marriages. Often, when tension exists between the spouse and family of origin, the power of the latter is formidable. This tends to be more true when it is daughter-in-law versus parent-in-law. The husband-son more often than not sides with his parents. Tension of this type is sometimes incomprehensible to Westerners, as is reflected in the omission of family-related items in the questionnaire. To most Westerners, one's family of origin is not even in the picture when it comes to marriage. For the Chinese Americans I have treated, romantic love is, of course, highly desirable and longed for, especially when one is as young as the subjects in the research study. Even at this stage, I noticed in my psychotherapy practice, the issue of how well the future mate meets family expectations is a concern, one carefully monitored and causing apprehension.

THE GREAT WALL MENTALITY: BOUNDARY AS REFLECTED IN DWELLINGS

A few years ago, a friend who had recently come from Shanghai asked me why American colleges and universities do not have a *damen,* a formal front gate, and walls around them: "Anyone can get in from anywhere." I was temporarily stunned: what gate? With his explanations I recalled, yes, there was always a wall surrounding the schools I attended, with a front gate for entrance that can be closed and locked. The same is also true for residences. A walled compound enclosing a *da jiating,* large family, is frequently featured in novels and movies about Chinese life. The "large family" is usually translated by Westerners as "extended family." From the Chinese perspective, a grandfather living in the same compound with his married sons' families and unmarried sons and daughters does not represent an "extension." It is the original whole.

There are numerous variations of such enclosures. Shanghai has "alleys," or *nongtang.* These are lines of homes sprawling out after one enters from the central gate, and the entire "unit" is enclosed by a long wall. Beijing's equivalent is called *hutong,* with the same formal gate and wall around the cluster of homes. Residents in *nongtang* or *hutong* are not families or even related. However, they are neighbors who often become surrogate families, addressing one another with familial titles. Since Chinese are not as mobile as Americans, these surrogate "families" can be together for a lifetime. Some of these traditional patterns are now being replaced by Western-style high-rise apartment buildings that, interestingly enough, are also "enclosed" by nature of their heights. The difference is that Chinese apartment-building neighbors are much more intermingled than Americans, who may not even know the name of a next-door neighbor after years of living side by side. When one travels in China's countryside, one sees even modest "mud" houses with some kind of a wall surrounding them. And, of course, there is the Great Wall to protect the entire country from the "barbarians" in the North.

These walls and formal gates clearly represent the Chinese position of central control of who is an insider, a *zijiren,* "self-person," and who is an outsider, *wairen,* to be kept out. Each enclosure contains layers of smaller "units" that are, in turn, controlled by the appropriate head of the household. In the United States one finds the legislature actively participating, for example, in problems regarding teenage smoking, pregnancy, or crime. In China, unquestionably, the families deal with such issues within their walls. In counseling parents accused of child abuse, one sees the utter frustration of new immigrant Chinese parents who are suddenly forbidden to discipline their children as they used to do. The traditional Chinese approach has sometimes been criticized by the West as being too rigid, harsh, and authoritarian. On the other hand, when the shooting in Jonesboro, Arkansas, involving an eleven-year-old and a thirteen-year-old who shot and killed five persons, happened in 1998, the well-known Harvard pediatrician Dr. T. Berry Brazelton described American youth as "isolated and very angry."

The United States and China are said to represent the two diametrically opposed concepts of individualism and interdependence. We can see problems in both. The Chinese overlap and interact with one another primarily within the "enclosures," as symbolized by their architecture. Their personal "expansions" tend to occur in more familiar and "official" settings, such as schools and workplaces, or through friends and families. These places, then, become part of their inner circle. Americans, on the other hand, interact with the outside world directly from their nuclear homes. Television talk shows are full of individuals broadcasting personal matters to the whole world. Western personal "expansions" have a wider scope and are more impersonal in nature. This cultural difference is translated into intergenerational conflicts between young Chinese Americans and their parents. Although the young wish to expand like "everybody else" around them, they are, however, without role models or support from their parents. The parents, coming from their own experience, often discourage them and are made anxious by "Western ways." We see these discrepancies turn into hurt feelings, disappointment, betrayal, and loneliness on the parents' part, and the younger generation experiences anger, confusion, and inferiority feelings for being socially "backward."

I used architectural symbolism here to show how the older generation's worldviews are deeply rooted in some fundamental aspects of their lives, without their conscious awareness. Unaware that their preferences are cultural differences and, therefore, arbitrary and relative, the parents may see their worldviews as absolute and the only alternative. Likewise, the young, being exposed only to Western ways, think what they are familiar with is the only option and do not see the cultural relativity either. Ethnocentricity is certainly not a unique feature limited to Chinese Americans or immigrants. We need only to look around and listen or even examine each of our own views to see the bias that whatever one is used to must be the only way, the right way. This universal human idiosyncrasy is at the root of most of the troubles in the world among individuals as well as among groups. It takes an exceptional person and exceptional effort to see another person's perspective.

In this chapter, I attempted to present an overview of a Chinese personal world and contrast it with that of an American personal world. The differences are vast. In this complex and nebulous region of East meets West, young Chinese Americans try to develop a sense of personal identity, which is the theme of the next chapter.

Chapter 2

The Environment
for Chinese-American Self-Identity

"I don't know who I am or what I am"; "I don't fit anywhere"; "I feel I'm invisible": these are phrases often spoken by young Chinese Americans. An American-born Chinese complained, when she was about to make her first trip to China, "Why do people keep on saying to me, 'It's nice you are going back to China'? I've never been there, so how can I 'go back'?"

This chapter addresses the process of self-identification, emphasizing factors, to be developed throughout the book, that are particularly salient to Chinese Americans. It is understood that the "self" is formed in the interactions between innate attributes, such as physical features, temperament, native intelligence and talents, and the external environment, a nature-nurture combination.

THE PROCESS OF SELF-IDENTIFICATION

When Snow White's wicked stepmother repeatedly asks the mirror who is the most beautiful woman of all, she is trying to form a sense of herself based on the feedback from the mirror. Likewise, we begin forming a sense of "Who I am" largely based on internalization of reflections and feedback from other people. We see ourselves as others see us. This process starts from the moment we are born. The "others" constitute these "mirrors." As with real mirrors, some are clear and accurate, and others are distorted to flatter or ridicule. Some mirrors are well-framed and in one piece and others are cracked, yellowing, or missing pieces. We encounter countless "mirrors" in a lifetime, or even in the course of one day. If, in the early years of one's life, the reflections and feedback provided a healthy and well-integrated sense of self, that person would be in a better position to weather the adversities later in life. As we mature, this kind of mirroring becomes more complex and not just dependent on other people. Certain nonpeople experiences can be just as meaningful.

Chinese-American anthropologist Francis L. K. Hsu (1971), in his concept of psychosocial homeostasis, uses insights from Chinese culture to offer a more precise formulation of how we live as social and cultural beings. In his formulation, Hsu takes into account all elements of human existence, including the unconscious, as well as both intimate and remote cultures and societies, actual and symbolic, with different degrees of relevance to each person.

From the West we can find a similar orientation in self-psychology, which is a branch of psychoanalysis as developed by Heinz Kohut. This school acknowledges the pivotal role of the interdependent environment in which we live instead of only focusing on unconscious and intrapsychic conflicts. Through the parents and other members of the extended family, cultural values are transmitted to a child's self-image. Of course, the specific content of these "transmissions" differs from culture to culture.

With these basic guidelines in mind, we may now take a look at the self-formation of Chinese Americans.

CHINESE-AMERICAN SELF-IDENTITY

When people, including Chinese Americans, say "Americans," they usually mean white Americans. It is as though even Native Americans and Chinese whose forefathers helped to build the railroad in the last century were less "American" than a first-generation European. At the 1998 Winter Olympic Games, which I mentioned in the last chapter, one of the American skaters, Michelle Kwan, a Chinese American, was expected to win the gold medal. Instead, a Caucasian-American skater, Tara Lipinski, did. MSNBC posted on its Web site the headline "American beats out Kwan." Politics aside, the psychological implications are profound. Many of the Chinese Americans I listened to in therapy recalled, as children, that they wanted to be "like everybody else." What they meant was to be like white people. It is ingrained in our society that the white race is the criterion by which everyone else is judged. One young woman recalls seeing cosmetic advertisements showing large, double-eyelid round eyes as examples of what "beauty" is; narrow single-eyelid eyes, on the other hand, were presented as being unattractive and in need of the cosmetic enhancement featured in the ads. Having internalized these standards of "beauty," many Asian women of all ages blacken areas around their eyes to make them look deeper and rounder. Confusion is inevitable when one lives in the cross section of East and West. Chinese Americans must sort out the contributing factors from both sides in the self-identification process.

Chinese Circumstances, American Circumstances

Two types of Chinese pioneers came to the United States beginning in the midnineteenth century.

On January 4, 1847, a nineteen-year-old Chinese youth named Yung Wing boarded a cargo ship, *Huntress,* at Guangzhou (Canton). He arrived in New York after ninety-eight days on the ocean to study at Yale University. He was the first Chinese *liu xuesheng,* overseas student. Upon returning to China in 1854 with a diploma from Yale, Yung spearheaded the first wave of Chinese youth between the ages of twelve and fifteen to come to America to study. These young students were selected from all over China. They had to be scholastically superior to pass the examinations for the government to fund their overseas studies. Others were sufficiently well-off to fund themselves. Many of these earlier overseas students who arrived before World War II became leaders in China, both in intellectual pursuits and in business. With numerous interruptions and variations, this exchange continues to this day (Qian, 1996).

The second wave of Chinese pioneers to come to America, especially to California, began in 1848; most were from the Pearl River delta of Guangdong Province, a coastal location in southern China, where the people were familiar with the sea and foreign traders. Due to natural calamities, repeated political upheavals, and consequences of the Opium Wars (1839-1842 and 1856-1860), these peasants were economically devastated (Fairbank, 1992; Nee and Nee, 1972; Yung, 1995). In the meantime, gold was discovered in California in 1848, which attracted many of these Chinese men. In the 1860s, thousands of Chinese were recruited for the construction of the Transcontinental Railroad. By 1880, the Chinese population in the United States reached 105,000. They made up 10 percent of California's population (The Repeal and Its Legacy, 1993). These men hoped to improve their financial situations to support their families back home through hard labor and bachelor lifestyles, even though many of them were married. Women were noticeably absent during these early years. For example, in 1855, women made up less than 2 percent of the total Chinese population in the United States (Yung, 1995). These Chinese men worked long hours at jobs that were exhausting and physically dangerous because few white men were willing to perform such work. They were often subject to physical and verbal abuse in their lives. In the following years, because of economic and racial pressures, more taxes were levied on the Chinese. They were also deprived of basic civil rights, such as the right to have family members immigrate to the United States, to give testimony in courts, to own land, or to have jobs in public works. In San Francisco, to step out of Chinatown was a risk (Nee and Nee, 1972; Yung, 1995). A Chinese man in his fifties told me tales of his grandfather being taunted by white men and youths outside of Chinatown, who would detain the man by wrapping his long queue around a lamppost.

Finally, the Chinese Exclusion Act of 1882 was passed, the only American immigration law based purely on racial discrimination. This law did not apply to Chinese students and merchants; it was used to limit Chinese laborers entering the United States and to keep their families in China from coming to join them. The most important aspect in relation to the theme of this book is the breakdown of Chinese families, which has far-reaching consequences even to this day. For example, it is not uncommon for some young Chinese Americans to tell me of their vague impressions that their grandfathers, fathers, and other male relatives had traveled back and forth between the two countries. These men went to China to marry and have children, only to be separated for many years while working in the United States. In other words, many of the parents of the young people themselves were from incomplete, single-parent families in which misfortune and poverty were abundant. The Exclusion Act was repealed in 1943 when China and the United States became allies in World War II. The practice of marrying and having children in China continued even after the repeal, primarily for financial reasons. Thus, disrupted family life over several generations is a common experience in Chinese-American families.

This brief overview of Chinese origins in America highlights the great suffering and humiliation, but also the endurance and courage, among the forefathers of many of the young Chinese Americans I now see in my office. This harsh history contributed to self-identity confusion for generations to come.

One Part of the Mirror: Chinese Familial Input

"I don't know anything about my parents' background. It's all in the dark. They don't talk about it" is a frequent comment I hear from young Chinese Americans, as though there is a conspiracy between the generations. Both agree to keep the past untouched. This phenomenon is well known among Holocaust and World War II Japanese-American internment camp survivors. Pain and humiliation are experiences no one wants either to remember or pass on to the young.

Who are these parents? With few exceptions, all parents of the young people in psychotherapy with me are immigrants. A few, even though American-born, are extremely "traditional" in their interactions with the world. Most of these parents are in their fifties and sixties. Their educational levels range from no schooling to doctorates. The mothers, as a group, have had less formal education than their spouses. This wide range in the educational background of these parents is still consistent with a 1997 study titled "Special Focus: Asian Pacific Americans Demographic and Educational Trends" (Hune and Chan, 1997). Fathers' occupations range from unskilled workers to professionals. Few of the mothers are professionals; many are homemakers. Some take in sewing or child care to supplement family income. Their children characterize them as being very traditional in their values, habits, and expectations. Even when they move out of the central Chinatown area, their activities are, by and large, restricted to the old circles. Most of them are limited in their knowledge of the English language. The language barrier between the generations is severe. The young people themselves began as monolingual, communicating only in Chinese. They dropped their first language upon entering school, because of both exposure and the desire to "fit in." They have all retained some Chinese to use with their parents in simple matters. Often, the children, at an early age, handled transactions with the outside world when

English was necessary. Role reversal is found in almost all of these Chinese-American families. As a sixty-year-old recent immigrant said, "Here [in the United States], I am deaf and dumb."

An additional problem related to the parents' English language deficit is that it is used and exploited in movies and novels about Chinese-American family life. In these representations, the parents are made to speak childlike, simplistic English with total disregard for grammar. In fact, many adult immigrants do speak in that fashion, which makes them appear ignorant and annoying. This, too, offends the children. On the other hand, if the children maintain their first language, they would view their parents as quite "normal." Perhaps, in movies about Chinese-American families, the parents can speak only in their native language, with English subtitles to convey their thoughts and ideas. This correction can help to earn them the respect they deserve.

In some families, the immigrant parents may practice certain traditional Chinese rituals during Chinese holidays or events such as weddings and funerals. I have heard several complaints from young Chinese Americans regarding their experiences at family funerals. As ancestor worship is still honored in some of the homes, deaths are often memorialized with loud wailing to show the deceased is blessed by grateful and filial descendents. In China, there were, perhaps still are in some rural areas, professional "mourners" who were hired to wail at a funeral, especially that of an elder. In contrast, we may recall that Mrs. John Kennedy was widely praised for her stoic calm at the long official ceremonies after President Kennedy's assassination. The young Chinese Americans are, for the most part, ignorant of the meanings of these rituals because their parents did not teach them. The end result is that the young, seeing how these practices differ from mainstream America, conclude their Chinese parents are "weird" and "backward." For the parents, these rituals are performed in a community that is unable to respond to the symbolic meanings. The experience is, therefore, unsatisfactory for both generations.

Most of these parents were described to me as hardworking, frugal people who invested all their hopes in the children's formal education. After all, the children's achievement is the reason why these parents came to this country in the first place. Many of these families suffered from poverty in China and upon arrival in the United States.

Another unique feature in these families is that the grandparents are often a crucial part of the core family and are entrusted with child care. It would be difficult for Westerners to understand the degree of emotional loss, through death or immigration, that some of these young people still feel regarding their grandparents. As described in Chapter 1, in China, when faced with problems, one can seek advice and comfort from those with whom one is familiar and whom one trusts. These persons can be expected to be available throughout one's life to guarantee stability. Once in the United States, most families lose this support network. Going to a professional, a stranger, is just not done. To live "deaf and "dumb" with no one to assist you in a sea of disorientation can be painfully demoralizing.

A majority of these immigrant parents whom I have heard about through their children are ruled by fear. Their lifestyle is characterized by defensiveness. One must be on guard at all times against evil intentions and manipulations of "outsiders," meaning society at large. The children were told to distrust these "outsiders" and to stick with familiar settings. In other words, adventure and risk taking are discouraged. Money becomes of paramount importance as a source of "power" and security. This fear and caution concerning money is often passed on to the next generation. Considering these parents' life circumstances and experiences, such fear and insecurity are understandable. It is my impression that many of the parents suffer from degrees of depression, manifested in sad moods, withdrawal, irritability, and various physical symptoms. This is one way they communicate their inner burdens to their children, who react with frustration and helplessness.

Another somewhat mute but persistent characteristic of these immigrant parents, or Chinese parents everywhere, is the importance of food. Related to this aspect of their daily lives is the central concern for health. Here, we are faced with a complex cultural difference. In Chinese conceptualization there is no body-mind dichotomy. From their language usage, it is clear that the body is the totality of the "self" (Tung, 1994). (This topic will be discussed further in Chapter 4, on the communication of emotions.) American-raised children frequently complain about the persistent emphasis on food, again not knowing its meaning. They wish their parents would talk to and understand them like the parents they see in television families. Instead, "All my mother does when I go home is to tell me to eat." Once more, behavior such as this causes the young to see their parents as ignorant and "so Chinesey." Complaints and criticisms of the parents are almost always accompanied by guilty feelings and profound helplessness. The young do not want to "betray" the parents by bad-mouthing them, yet they cannot understand or solve these problems.

From my observations, there seems to be a basic difference between the American-born and the China-born (including Taiwan and Hong Kong) youth regarding self-identity. If migration takes place after the children's memory is stabilized, usually by ten or twelve years of age, and especially if the Chinese language is maintained, the young immigrants may not suffer from that fundamental identity confusion. They may be homesick, feel like misfits, as if they are alienated and "homeless," but they know they are Chinese who now live in America. For those who came from mainland China after 1949 when the People's Republic of China was established, their being able to "go home" now further solidifies their sense of identity. As one middle-aged woman said, to emigrate from China for political reasons felt like an "emotional amputation." A certain amount of healing became possible after the normalization of the relationship between the two countries, as will be addressed in Chapter 5 on the integration process.

Another Part of the Mirror: American Reflections

A number of Chinese-American young men told me about being picked last in sports and games in school, and one said, sarcastically, "I'd be picked first if it were in math." He happened to be an athletic person uninterested in mathematics. I have also worked with a few mixed-race couples, mostly white men with Chinese wives. The men spoke no Chinese and the women spoke very little English. As the sessions progressed, it became clear that the men assumed they were marrying docile, obedient, and sexy Chinese women who would make no demands on them. The wives in these cases married for pragmatic reasons—to make a living. These stereotypes did not come about overnight. Movies made in the early years of Hollywood always showed Chinese women as mysterious, sly, but beautiful in a witchlike fashion. Chinese men were portrayed in movies as small, passive, and silent, with backs arched in ready apology. Of course, both Chinese men and women were inscrutable and spoke broken English. As recently as the March 24, 1997, cover of the *National Review,* President and Mrs. Clinton and Vice President Gore were depicted in a most unflattering caricature of Asian images, with protruding teeth, straw hats, and silly grins. These depictions, intentionally or unintentionally, made the Chinese appear either bad or inept, or both. Unfortunately, these are the messages internalized by many of the younger generation. Instead of seeing themselves and their parents as different, they interpreted these social clues as "Something is wrong with me."

When my family first came to the United States in the early 1950s, we lived in Berkeley, California. I remember overhearing the adults talking about how "For Rent" signs were posted on the buildings, but they were told the places were rented when they approached. I did not pay much attention to their conversation until I went house hunting with my father one day. To this day, I remember clearly a tall white woman in a brown house on then Grove Street and now Martin Luther King, Jr. Street. She looked at us in disbelief that quickly turned to anger, as if to say, "How dare you!" and slammed the door in our faces. I was in my teens. The house-hunting experiences left me surprised and then angry. Racial discrimination was not part of my preparation in coming to this country, but I soon understood the meaning in these encounters. Eventually my father was advised to place an ad in the paper indicating that a "Chinese professor's family" desired to rent a home. Several calls came in, and we moved into a house on Hopkins Street. The owners, the Carter family, lived in back of us. The two families became good friends. Berkeley, even fifty years ago, was an intelligent city. I wonder what it would be like to live in a more ignorant and discriminatory environment all my life, and if my family were less fortunate.

A Third Part of the Mirror: Cultural and Racial Distances

I have long been intrigued by how little babies seem to be keenly interested in other little babies. They just know they belong to the same club. Dogs, too, check out others of their own kind. Films on animal behavior show grouping behavior. Looking around the world one sees how a sense of commonality, be it racial, ethnic, religious, or political, inspires cooperation; it also triggers warfare more than any other motivation. To be "color blind" may only be advocated in legislative terms or in commercials. In reality, a line, a gap, does exist between groups—and that does not necessarily have to be bad. In the present context I am referring to what can be called a neutral indifference, a cultural and racial distance due more to lack of exposure and interest than to preconceived abhorrence or avoidance. That long-existing prejudices can lurk just beneath this indifference is granted. It is a matter of level of consciousness, intentionality, and interest that I am considering here.

Most Chinese Americans tend to befriend other Chinese Americans, at least in their inner circles. Their activities are also bounded by this parameter. The theme of racial interaction is touched upon within different contexts in this book. For the present, we shall stay with the phenomenon of general lack of exposure of Chinese Americans to the lives of other Americans. (The reverse is also true but not under present discussion.) What this restricted life space means is that these Chinese Americans simply do not have as much information and skills to negotiate in a society that is dominated by the mainstream culture. Judgment of "fairness" aside, we are talking about missed opportunities. Their "repertoire" in life could be broadened to their benefit. Being bicultural can mean one is well versed in both cultures. Certain activities in our daily lives may bring about exchange and mutual familiarity. For example, a young Chinese-American father took his family to a performance of the annual holiday offering of *The Nutcracker,* their first visit to the San Francisco Memorial Opera House and to a ballet. Though he did not particularly appreciate the dancing, he did enjoy chatting about the event with his co-workers the next day as a shared experience. In another case, a Chinese-American mother succeeded in having her children's teachers pencil in major Chinese holidays on the classroom calenders alongside the other holidays and went to the classes with appropriate stories and treats when the Chinese holidays arrived.

In choosing a profession, Chinese Americans tend to go into non-people-oriented careers, even though the horizon is broadening gradually today. For example, in 1997, the 105-year-old American Psychological Association elected its first Asian American, a Chinese American, as the association president. Out of a membership of 100,000, only about 1,000 are Asian Americans. My own route to becoming a clinical psychologist illustrates how choice is narrowed due to lack of exposure.

In my sophomore year at the University of California at Berkeley in the early 1950s, I had to declare a major. I had no idea what I wanted to do except that I did not want to work with people. I was limited by a severe language deficiency and generally felt like a foreigner, having been in this country for only a couple years. My parents, unlike most Chinese parents, never pressured me or my siblings to pursue any particular occupation. Most of my fellow Chinese students were studying engineering or life and physical sciences. (This pattern still holds true, according to Hune and Chan, 1997.) I knew I did not want to work in any of these fields.

One day, I attended a talk by the principal of the California School for the Deaf. He mentioned that he had majored in child psychology and that it had been a rewarding profession for him. That was the first time I heard the word "psychology," but only in connection with becoming a teacher for the deaf. That option was more palatable than all the others, so I decided to major in psychology, with no idea what the field was about. Upon graduation I applied to a training institute for teachers of the deaf as a part-time student, as I needed to work to support myself. "No," came the response; the institute did not accept part-time students. That such a turn of events did not upset me was an indication of my ambivalence about becoming a teacher for the deaf.

I worked for a couple of years in offices performing clerical jobs. Then, purely by chance, through a friend, I found a position as a psychometrician at the Institute for Psychological Services at the Illinois Institute of Technology in Chicago. Among our responsibilities was interviewing clients who either were seeking vocational counseling or were applicants for high-level positions sent to us for additional evaluation. After group and individual testing, the psychometricians did an information-collecting interview and the clients would then be seen by the counseling psychologists at a later date. I thought nothing of our activities until a fellow psychometrician remarked on how good my interviews were. I was puzzled: doesn't everybody do them the same way? Also while working at this setting, I heard terms such as psychotherapy, psychoanalysis, clinical psychology, etc. They sounded like foreign countries to me. I could relate them to nothing in my background. One afternoon I was told the counseling psychologist, Dr. Kulick, wanted to see me. When I went to his office he was smiling and chatty: Had I thought of going to graduate school for an advanced degree in psychology? He had noticed how good my interviews were and felt I had the talent to become a psychologist. "The only trouble is," Dr. K. chuckled, "after talking to you, the clients don't want to talk to me anymore!"

I returned to San Francisco and started in the master of science in clinical psychology program at then San Francisco State College, now University. To this day, I consider the three years I spent there my significant learning period. Both in the classes and among my fellow students, "psychotherapy" was a big item. It was believed that a prerequisite to becoming a clinician is the experience of personal psychotherapy. I thought I would give it a try, maybe for a couple of months during summer vacation. I was hooked in the first session after my therapist, the phenomenologist Ludwig Lefebre, interpreted what he called a "transference dream" I had the night before. Looking back, my becoming a psychologist was a peculiar journey in an alien territory. Each step was unexpected and unplanned. I either rejected or followed a thread purely based on intuition. I could not really plan, for example, to go directly to a doctoral program because I did not know where I was supposed to "go." I knew more about what I did not want to do. I was not interested in being in the academic world. After the master's program, "equipped" with an uncharted map, I went to Kansas because I wanted a "real" clinical experience. The original plan was to stay one year. Instead, I remained there for four and a half years. Professionally, this period gave me the knowledge and experience to ground and orient myself. I eventually obtained a doctorate for practical purposes, to have more freedom in doing what is important to me. Now, thirty-five years later, I still cannot think of anything else I would rather do.

"E.T. PHONE HOME":
ROOTS OF THE "SELF"

Yet another aspect to the sense of one's "self" is rarely, if ever, discussed but is most fundamental and ever present.

The adorable extraterrestrial visitor E.T. won our hearts for his endearing qualities. We felt sad when he was homesick, wanted to call home, and eventually left us to go home. Likewise, when we travel, we want to send postcards, call home, and FAX messages to "touch base" with persons and places where we are "from." We talk about "baseline" and "bottom line" to stabilize and orient ourselves. When something is said to be "groundless," we mean that thing does not really exist. When a speaker's view is "well grounded," we can trust it because the view is firmly rooted and therefore credible. We consider essential a person's "background" in understanding this person's totality. These everyday expressions point to the absolute necessity for a sense of continuity, permanence, belonging, and certainty in one's "being." We all need clear knowledge of where we are from, as in the expression "I know/don't know where you are coming from." Where we are from defines our place in the world. We are all historically connected to someone and somewhere.

When one's "background" or "baseline" is cut off, in harm's way, or uncertain, this affects a person's sense of "being real." This basic phenomenology is very much in operation for immigrants, especially those who immigrated for reasons that prevented their going back or, as in the case of African Americans, who were kidnapped by force. E.T. was fortunate: he had a home he could call and a spaceship to take him there. He also lives in our hearts on planet Earth. (This theme will be readdressed in Chapter 5 on integration.)

In presenting these segments of the "mirror" for Chinese-American identity, I hope to show that a cohesive self-identity for members of a minority is extremely difficult to achieve because of the fragmentation. To see an integrated reflection of the "self," one needs a mirror that is unified and accurate. However, I believe that the degree of integration can be much improved through openness and a raised level of awareness. Both immigrant families and society must work together in building a bridge that can interpret alien behavior into meaningful human commonality.

Chapter 3

"You Have a Chinese What?!": Internalized Inferiority

About twenty-five years ago, when I was on the staff of a psychiatric clinic, a young Chinese-American woman was assigned to me. I sensed she was reticent and unhappy about something that had to do with me. She eventually told me that upon hearing she had a Chinese therapist, her sisters reacted: "You have a Chinese WHAT?!" Implied in their disbelief was that she was given a second-class therapist.

It is true that psychotherapy originated in the West and twenty years ago there were very few qualified Asian therapists. Another possibility was that the sisters believed only a white therapist could help her. The theme of white authority has been repeatedly reinforced, for example, in movies in which a white person, usually a man, either suppressed unruly behavior or came to the rescue of people of color. During colonial rule, white people were in charge of the lives of colored locals. In addition, the principle of identification with the aggressor underscores the process by which the oppressed may perceive themselves as losers and the conqueror as the rightful superior.

In the previous chapter, I described how disruptive elements in an environment can confuse the process of self-identification. In this chapter, I will discuss social, cultural, and historical components of internalized inferiority feelings experienced by some Chinese Americans and even Chinese in China. These feelings, of course, may operate at different levels of awareness in each person.

"ASIANNESS AS A LIABILITY"

Joanna Su, the newly appointed director of the Advisory Council on Asian Affairs of Chicago, said she felt her Asianness was a liability while growing up in a white suburb of Detroit. "I was more or less embarrassed to be an Asian American." When her classmates pulled their eyelids to "slant" them or mocked Chinese language, she blamed herself for being "different" (Yip, 1997b). Gary Locke, the first Asian (Chinese)-American governor (of Washington State) in the United States, recalled a third-grade teacher who had asked the children each day what they had for breakfast. She would slap a child's hands whenever that child reported having what she considered "un-American" foods. "Experiences like those did take their toll, and a lot of my classmates with immigrant parents became embarrassed of our parents' cultures. We went overboard to become 110-percent American" (Locke, 1997, p. 7). Both Su and Locke, of course, moved far beyond these hurtful experiences to become what they are today.

I have heard "confessions" of feelings and thoughts similar to those of Su and Locke. These young people recall childhood experiences when they were called names, teased, chased on streets, and beaten up, while knowing that even their parents were helpless to protect them. Now, as adults, some of them still perceive their parents as socially inept and, therefore are reluctant to take them to Western-style restaurants or other places primarily frequented by white Americans. I have also been told how, socially, some of these young Chinese Americans feel more "protected" and "worthy" when they are in the company of white Americans, as if elevating their status. Others may go the opposite direction by keeping company only with other Chinese Americans. Still others keep trying both ways, hoping to find a good balance. All three "methods" leave them feeling incomplete.

SELF-PRESENTATION

Painful as these experiences are, the one area these young adults most frequently describe to me as agonizing is their self-presentation in social and professional settings. Since most of them have no knowledge of the cultural and social factors that conditioned them in their youth, they see such behavior patterns in absolute terms, that something is innately wrong with them. They may feel that they are ineffective in what they do, that people do not take them seriously, that they cannot express themselves as white people do, and they may be troubled by the thought "What is wrong with me?" These young people are well educated; some are very successful in their work. Yet, they feel inadequate in personal ways. In the following pages, I will examine cultural differences in socialization, gender differentiation, and gender preference, which all contribute to these feelings.

Cultural Differences in Socialization

Chinese-American anthropologist Frances Hsu writes:

> American schools foster a desire and a skill for self-expression that is little known in the Chinese schools. . . . When I compare American youngsters with those I have known in China, I cannot help being amazed at the ease and the self-composure of the former when facing a single listener or a sizable audience, as contrasted with the awkwardness and the self-consciousness of Chinese youngsters in similar circumstances. (Hsu, 1981, p. 93)

Hsu further elaborates that in interdependent cultures such as China and other Asian countries, children are expected to be sensitive to the environment, whereas in the American individualistic culture the children expect the environment to be sensitive to them. American children are encouraged to express themselves, to speak up. Chinese children are taught to get along, to place others' needs before their own. Chinese children are told frequently to *ting hua,* literally, to listen to the speech (of an adult). These rules of behavior become deeply ingrained and are carried into adulthood outside of the home. Of course, these are the cultural values that individuals strive toward, with various degrees of success. Not all Chinese are modest, and not all white Americans are assertive.

A good way to learn about a culture is to listen to its proverbs and sayings. Chinese culture is particularly rich in this respect. We will look at a few that warn against being too visible, against going it alone. One of the best known is

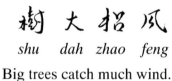

shu   dah   zhao   feng

Big trees catch much wind.

This saying relates to being on top and out on a limb, a risky business. In cultures that respect hierarchical order, to stand out is disruptive. In relation to the Chinese-American population under discussion, we must also remember, as described in Chapter 2, many of the parents were uncommunicative in the American sense. The children grew up in an atmosphere that considered speaking up to be potentially dangerous or harmful, as in the saying

bing   cong   kou   ru,   huo   cong   kou   chu

Disease enters through the mouth.

Disaster comes out from the mouth.

Harmony is to be preserved above all else by being careful about what one says.

When we speak of self-presentation we are actually looking at how a person relates to his or her surroundings. Once I gave a fortieth-birthday card to a friend that had a simple line to indicate a hill. A little man is tumbling down the hill, in shock. On the inside the script reads, "After 40 it's all downhill." In America, we do not like a downhill slide, nor do we like an uphill struggle. The only accepted position in relation to a hill, or any other situation in life, is to be "on top." Yet, we also say "lonely at the top." These are the two sides of the individualism coin. Western civilization is full of accounts of "going all the way" drive and expansionism. Whether it is Mt. Everest, supersonic cars, the Wild West, or colonialism, something always has to be conquered, to reach the top. Westerners are not afraid to do what the Chinese call

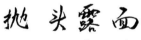

puo   tou   lu   mian

thrust one's head out (to) expose one's face

or to become conspicuous. They thrive on being the first or the only one in a new venture. They assume they are entitled wherever they go. They simply make themselves at home.

On the other hand, the position that one is to be sensitive and adjust to the environment is so well ingrained in Asians that a thoughtful person will not put another person in the predicament of compromising this understanding. This contrast is well described by Doi, one of the first Japanese psychiatrists who came to the United States for professional training following World War II. Shortly after arriving in 1950, which was only a few years after the war, while visiting an American home, he was asked by the host if he was hungry. He was, but, being Japanese, he denied it, hoping the host would ask again, as would a Japanese host. The host did not. "And I found myself thinking that a Japanese would almost never ask a stranger unceremoniously if he was hungry, but would produce something to give him without asking" (Doi, 1981, p. 11). He then described how many questions he was asked during the visit: what kind of drink before dinner? tea or coffee after dinner? and with or without cream and sugar? etc. He associated the usual "Please help yourself" with the uncomfortable thought "Nobody else will help you" (p. 13).

To be personally attentive is a valued interpersonal behavior in Chinese and other Asian cultures. Once I received a letter from a social worker who had just come from Beijing, posted from Oakland, about twenty miles across the Bay. In the letter she apologized for writing instead of visiting me in person. She actually had come to my residence twice but did not find me home. Since she did not have my telephone number she could not call. She also enclosed a letter of introduction from a mutual friend. When we finally met in person we discussed the cultural differences in circumstances such as this one. It would be considered rude in America to suddenly show up on someone's doorstep. To the Chinese, a mailed letter of introduction would be too impersonal and, therefore, rude. Taking the trouble to visit in person expresses sincerity and respect.

Similar to Doi's experience in his early days in the United States, I have been asked by several visiting Chinese psychologists, "Why do the Americans have to ask if you want something?" A Chinese American invited one of the visitors to a movie by asking if he wanted to go. He said no, smiling. I happened to be there and witnessed the cross-cultural misunderstanding. I knew he really wanted to go but could not bring himself to say so. It is not "proper." Another visiting psychologist called to consult with me one day. His host had asked if he wanted to go to Lake Tahoe. "Why do Americans always have to ask?" "Do you want to go?" I asked him. "Yes." "Then tell him

'Yes'." Since both these Chinese psychologists were part of a cross-cultural exchange program, I explained the cultural differences to them.

For Americans, questions imply the person has a choice and is in control of her or his circumstances. That the Chinese do not ask, but simply assume, does not mean the guest's wishes are not honored. It means the other person is not to be put on the spot, since the host should already know what is usually expected under the circumstances. In case of uncertainty, one simply offers what is customarily considered appropriate. This assumption is different from empathy; it is more a culturally choreographed interaction, enacted repeatedly. In this manner, without having to say a word, the Asian person's needs are met. To the Chinese, questions only imply insincerity and reluctance. Here, we are dealing with what anthropologists refer to as "level of context." When a group of people have shared experiences, they need only a few words to convey an idea to others to be understood. This phenomenon was beautifully portrayed by Akira Kurosawa, the gifted Japanese film director, in his film *Rhapsody in August.* The central figure is an elderly grandmother who had experienced tragic losses during the August 1945 bombing of Nagasaki. Her grandchildren were visiting on yet another memorial of that August day. These Westernized grandchildren are light-years away from that experience and unable to appreciate their grandmother's preoccupation. One day her old friend, another elderly victim from that fateful day, came to visit. The camera focuses on them from a distance, through the open door. We see these two frail little old women sitting on the floor mat, facing each other, motionless and in complete silence. When her friend left the grandmother was all smiles, saying to her grandchildren, "We had a nice chat." When the level of shared experience is that high, words become superfluous. Generally speaking, the level of context, or shared experience, is much higher in an interdependent culture than in an individualistic one. This is one reason why Asians usually do not value or trust verbal communication. It is action, or behavior, that counts.

To try to act other than how one has been brought up to act can be difficult, even immobilizing or tormenting to the person. An early personal experience of mine demonstrates this. After graduating from college with a bachelor's degree in psychology in the late 1950s, I could find no employment with such a low-level degree in the field. Not knowing what I was supposed to do with psychology anyway, I looked for office work in San Francisco. I felt discouraged after being turned down by a few prospective employers. I knew that I needed to act more "American": positive and confident. Should I tell them I have experience doing similar work when I do not? I finally decided at least to sound "positive and confident." The very first interview in which I said, "Yes, I learn very fast, and I'm a good worker" I was hired. This job paid better wages than all the others for which I had been turned down. I received a raise long before the promised six months, as well as repayment of 50 percent of the fee I had paid the employment agency. Despite these "gains," I felt horrible inside. I felt I had "sold out." For a long time I suffered the sadness and guilt of "self-betrayal." No one could help me to process the conflicts, explain to me that it is necessary sometimes to act in a way that the other party can "understand." Just as one speaks English to an English-speaking person and Chinese to a Chinese-speaking person, so it is with behavior. No betrayal is involved. This experience made an impression on me when I finally understood it. It helped me to appreciate the psychological difficulties in "cultural conversion."

A few years ago, at a restaurant, I overheard a young white woman telling her friend about her job interview: "I told them they are lucky to have me." I smiled and recalled my own, very different, experience. Even though I was not actually suffering from internalized inferiority, my behavior would be perceived by Westerners as lacking in self-confidence. At least, being from

China, I was aware of the cultural difference. In China, employment negotiations are conducted through "connections," mutual acquaintances who can vouch for your qualifications so that you do not have to "boast" for yourself.

Another conflict Chinese Americans have discussed with me is their embarrassment when paid a compliment. They know they are supposed to be gracious about it, but they just feel awkward. Again, this is merely another reflection of the cultural value of not being conspicuous and conceited. When a Chinese is given praise she or he should deflect the compliment. This does not mean that compliments should not be paid. Westerners have asked me if they would actually offend a Chinese by their praise. With the Chinese, even compliments are shared. This is why when Chinese leaders are being applauded they applaud back. In other words, whereas Westerners do not hesitate to stand out as winners, the Chinese demur to group cohesion. They do let their hair down, however, when they are with their "in" group, as is consistent with their sense of boundary.

Cultural Differences in Gender Differentiation: The Case for Men

Two of the most common difficulties expressed by the Chinese-American young men with whom I worked are the feeling that they are not attractive to women and the heavy burden they carry in relation to their parents. In the former case, they think Chinese-American women prefer white men. They attribute this to their not being aggressive enough and to their smaller physical stature. This perception causes them to feel even less confident. In the latter case, responsibility to their parents can be hard to bear. Because of the value placed on sons in Chinese families, these young men have been conditioned to feel obligated to realize parental expectations. As with practically everything else in American and Chinese cultures, gender roles are clearly different.

In 1993, when I was consulting at the Clinical Psychology Research Center of Hunan Medical University in China, I witnessed something that both intrigued me and taught me an important lesson. Several Chinese colleagues and I were having dinner at a rather large, but quiet, restaurant. Gradually I noticed, across the room, a party of about twenty young men. I noticed them because their noise level was steadily increasing. A few of them, wine glasses in hand, were walking around the two tables they occupied to "invite" specific individuals to take a drink. (To the Chinese, drinking is a social activity, a time for intense interaction. One does not simply take a drink. One is either "invited" to take a drink with someone, or one does the inviting. Games are also played in which the loser takes the "penalty" and drinks.) Initially, quite a few of them were engaged in this activity, but the number gradually decreased. I also noticed that one particular young man in a white shirt made the rounds continuously. Eventually, only three of them were still "in," but the noise level increased even more. Then, only one was left, the young man in the white shirt, still standing, smiling, unaffected. Not knowing exactly what they were doing, I nevertheless felt impressed by this young man, although he had no obvious physical characteristics to attract attention. I realized that I sensed his superiority, not because he lasted longer than the others, but because of his easy composure.

I mentioned my observations to my Chinese colleagues. "Oh, yes," they said. "The enactment is called *jiu wenhua,* wine culture, a male ritual." We then discussed the topic of the Chinese sense of masculinity. The masculine man to the Chinese is not an athlete, a Don Juan, or a social extrovert. Good looks and big muscles not only are not prerequisites but can be liabilities. The Chinese sense of masculinity stresses a man's character, brains (one is wise, not just clever), articulation, and leadership qualities. In *jiu wenhua,* the "real man" not only can hold down more liquor than others, he does so easily, with his head clear and his character intact. The young man in the white shirt gave me that impression.

What I learned from my Chinese colleagues is perfectly consistent with portrayals of *yingxiong haohan,* heroes and "real men," in Chinese classics such as *Sanguo Yangyi,* which has been translated into English as *Romance of Three Kingdoms,* and *Shui Hu Zhuan, All Men Are Brothers.* These men have proved themselves, repeatedly, to be honorable, wise, courageous, filial, and superior in martial arts. Their moral character, in the end, is what distinguishes them from the ordinary. They speak only at crucial times, and then they speak wisely and effectively. They are also differentiated by the quality of *yi,* which has no English equivalent but implies loyalty, honor, integrity, reciprocity, and male bonding (not always necessary). An act of *yi* is assumed to be carried out at great personal risk and expense.

As we can see, the Chinese definition of manhood is quite different from that of the West. The former emphasizes qualities not immediately evident. By definition, the Chinese man should not be conspicuous. In American culture, an inward emphasis is often seen as being passive, meek, and submissive. Furthermore, Chinese culture is more interpersonal and interactional, requiring deference that, by traditional American standards, is considered more in the "feminine" sphere. In the context of our topic, internalized inferiority, a boy raised with these Chinese values would most likely have difficulties adjusting to the more aggressive Western norms, especially if cultural differences were not explained to him. Many of these young men grew up with fathers who were, in actuality, helpless and depressed. Family circumstances compound traditional Chinese coping styles, making East-West integration even more burdensome to the young.

At this point, I would like to relate another anecdote and quote an ancient text to show the timelessness of a cultural pattern.

In Golden Gate Park of San Francisco, by a lake, groups of students of tai chi and other Eastern martial arts practice early in the morning on weekends. Here, one sees the best example of harmonious diversity. Persons of all ages, sexes, and colors, move silently in graceful unison. Seagulls and pigeons share the warm sun with humans without fear. Once I decided to walk around the lake to observe the different groups. Although not much verbal instruction is used, I came upon a teacher of one small group who was saying to the students that one should never be "stronger" or more forceful than one's opponent. Instead, one remains observant of the opponent, waiting for her or his weak moment, and wins with ease. Related to this lesson is the following passage from Sun Tzu's classic *The Art of Strategy* (1988), written more than twenty-three centuries ago:

THE TRIUMPH OF NO EFFORT

Those who are aware of triumph
When it is obvious also to the multitudes,
Do not have excellent skills.

Those who triumph during conflict
While the world says, "Well done!"
Do not have excellent skills.

To lift an autumn leaf is not an act of great strength.
To see the sun and moon is not an act of sharp sight.
To hear a sudden thunderclap is not an act of acute listening.

Those whom the Ancient Ones called "Skilled in conflicts"
Are those who triumph because triumph is easy.

Gender Preference in Chinese Culture: The Case for Women

Cultural differences in gender differentiation for women are just as profound, if not more so. An emphasis on inward qualities becomes more restrictive for them. Modesty, chastity, thought-fulness, and willingness to take a backseat to their brothers are assumed. In addition to these traditional Chinese values, women also suffer from gender preference. Almost without exception, the young Chinese (and other Asian)-American women I have seen in psychotherapy spoke of gender preferences in their families as pervasive and powerful. Judy Yung, in her book *Unbound Feet,* wrote about her own experiences: "My brother, Warren, always got the best servings of food at the dinner table. He had his own tricycle, while we five sisters shared a single pair of roller skates" (1995, p. 287). Whereas the brother was expected to finish college and become a doctor, the parents felt it enough for the daughters to finish high school and marry well. Implied here is the tremendous pressure Chinese sons have to live with and the "opaque" ceiling Chinese daughters live under. After all, for ages, Chinese mothers have admonished their daughters that

女子姦材便是徳
nuzi   wu   cai   bian   shi   de

the absence of talent is a virtue for a woman.

In my office, I have heard many similar stories. Too frequently, mothers of these young people were, themselves, victims of gender abuse. This is an open practice because such behavior is culturally condoned, a matter of "common sense." These young women were on the receiving end of extensive familial criticism and condemnation simply because they were not sons. When a family had either no son or too many daughters, the parents were looked down upon by relatives as having "failed." The anger, in turn, was sometimes turned against these daughters. As in Yung's experience, daughters are expected to take a backseat to their brothers. In recent years, couples and single women and men have been going to China to adopt baby girls, which is yet another reflection of this gender preference, as these baby girls are unwanted by their own families.

Since gender preference is a deep-seated tradition in Chinese culture, it may be worthwhile to take a look at data from China on gender imbalance.

A review essay on sexual behavior in modern China, a report of the nationwide "sex civilization" survey on 20,000 subjects in China, noted that 42.8 percent of Chinese female university students, who are the elite among Chinese women, indicated that they would prefer to be a male if they had a choice. Only 8.3 percent of their counterparts, the male university students, indicated such gender dysphoria. This study was conducted from 1989 to 1990 (Lau, 1995).

In a second study regarding sex differences in suicide rates in China, the authors stated that while the suicide rate among males is higher than that among females in most countries of the world, this picture is reversed in China. Data collected in China show the highest suicide rate is among females ages twenty to twenty-four. This group accounts for 45 percent of the total suicides (Zhao et al., 1994).

A third source is data from my 1993 visit to Hunan. The main vehicle for teaching was supervision of cases seen at the outpatient clinic staffed by Drs. Tang Quiping and Yang Jian. I soon noticed the high frequency and acuteness in patients' presenting complaints that would be diagnosed as social phobia in the United States. We decided to systematically record such incidents to verify this impression. A total of ninety-five cases were collected. Included in the "social phobia" group were patients who identified, in the initial visit, clear-cut symptoms while in interpersonal and social situations as the main reason for seeking counseling.

The ninety-five cases collected included forty-five women and fifty men. The age range was eighteen to fifty-three. Of these ninety-five cases, thirty-two, or 34 percent, met the criterion for inclusion in the "social phobia" group. In this target group, women outnumbered men twenty to twelve. Combining both sexes, only three individuals were older than thirty. The most frequent complaints of the target group included the fear that people may look down on them, that they may blush in social settings, or that they would otherwise become conspicuous because of their inadequacies. They often described themselves as shy, reclusive, clumsy, and generally unattractive. Acute anxiety in relation to the opposite sex was frequently mentioned. A few noted feeling inferior because they were from a rural background. Insomnia, depression, and suicidal ideation were common to this group. The small size of the study sample qualifies the study more as informational than as hard research data. The study's findings again point to the pattern of added burden on young Chinese women.

The theme of vulnerability of today's young Chinese women runs through all three studies. Here, we are looking at "personal worth," which is different from "self-worth." Although the latter is influenced by the former, self-worth is subjective, a matter of how one experiences oneself. Personal worth is a more culturally assigned value of how society at large sees a group of persons, such as in a case of discrimination. It is deeply rooted in tradition and often taken for granted as a given "reality" of life.

This absence of intrinsic personal worth of a daughter carries over even after her death. In certain parts of rural China, especially in the south, including Taiwan, there is a ceremony called *minghun,* or a wedding between a ghost and a man. When a female child dies early in life, a "wedding" ceremony is held at the time when she would have reached a marriageable age. The same is not necessary for a son because when a son is born, he is automatically "registered" in the family structure. A girl can only gain an official place in her husband's family. To appease her ghost, her family must marry her off. To find her a husband, they place a red envelope with money in it in a public place. When a man picks it up, he becomes the bridegroom, even if he is already married. Men do not turn down this opportunity because they wouldn't want to offend a ghost. Second, the "groom" will receive a dowry from the girl's family as he would in a real wedding (Lee, 1994).

To go further back, to the beginning of time, as it were, we have the myth of Nu Kua, the goddess credited for creating humans. Nu Kua is described as having the face of a human and the body of a serpent. The goddess changes form seventy times a day (Yuan and Chan, 1985). This creator goddess appeared early in Chinese mythical tradition, from fourth century B.C., "as an independent deity and a major cosmogonic goddess" (Birrell, 1993, p. 164). However, by the latter Han era (25-250 A.D.), she had become one of a number of minor deities. From there, she was further demoted to being a consort of a male god, and her creator status was given to the male god P'an Ku, who actually appeared in Chinese mythology some six centuries later (Birrell, 1993; Yuan and Chan, 1985). Quoting Edward Schafer, Birrell offers, "Her gradual degradation from her ancient eminence was partly due to the contempt of some eminent and educated men for animalian gods, and partly due to the increasing dominating of masculinity in the elite social doctrine" (1993, p. 164).

The information included in this section highlights the depth and breadth of the background behind the social presentation style of Chinese Americans. Appreciating the richness of the soil from which a particular behavior grows is a step toward appreciating the behavior itself.

YES, EVEN IN CHINA

The phenomenon of internalized inferiority in relation to Westerners, especially white Americans, is present even in today's China.

I returned to China in October 1979, after being away for twenty-eight years. I stayed in Shanghai both at the beginning and at the end of my seven-week trip. Upon arrival, I was assigned by the Chinese Travel Bureau to the Jin Jiang Hotel, considered the best grand old hotel of Shanghai at that time. On the third day, I was politely asked to change to another room because, I was told, they had made a mistake in their reservations. I thought nothing of it. The next day, I was again politely asked to change to another room. I took notice: What is going on? Another reservation mistake, I was told. I felt dubious. A young hotel employee walked by and whispered to me, "Only Chinese are asked to change rooms." Like a flash, the bad old days came back to me. We had seen this phenomenon in Shanghai before, when, after World War II, my family had moved there from Chongqing. We had also witnessed it in the few months we were in Hong Kong. This practice is not unusual in cities that were colonized by Westerners. Similarly, near the end of 1998 radio announcements proclaimed that Hong Kong's Cathay Airline would soon offer direct flights between Hong Kong and San Francisco. Even though Hong Kong was returned to China on July 1, 1997, after a century of British colonization, these announcements were made in English with a clean British accent.

Always, a certain segment of Chinese people looks down on their own. By identifying with Westerners, even as servants of Westerners, they feel they are superior by association. To these persons, being Chinese is indeed a liability. This is by no means a unique Chinese manifestation. One has only to read or view movies about British colonization of India, for example. This theme is widespread, and has been examined in-depth by Edward Said, for example, in his book *Culture and Imperialism* (1993). Prior to checking out of Jin Jiang Hotel, I wrote on the comment card, "If we Chinese want others to respect us, we must respect ourselves first."

The "soil" from which internalized inferiority grew has been recorded by Westerners. In her book *China Dreams: Growing Up Jewish in Tientsin,* Isabelle Maynard wrote about how her parents had fled Russia after the revolution, intending to emigrate to America, the "promised land." They ended up instead in what her father called "Godforsaken" China for twenty-five years. Maynard was born and lived in China until age nineteen, when her family came to the United States. She never learned the Chinese language. The only Chinese persons with whom she had regular contact were nameless, known only as "Amah" (maid), "Boy," or "Cook." "[We] were snubbed in China by the more prosperous and self-proclaimed high-status Americans, English, Germans, and French. . . . [We] alienated ourselves from the Chinese people by choice, snubbing them as we ourselves had been snubbed" (1996, p. xvii). Similar experiences in Tientsin were also recorded in the television program *Round Eyes in the Middle Kingdom* by Ron Levaco, aired on Public Television in the San Francisco area on October 23, 1997. The family lived in Tientsin's "British concession" while waiting to come to the United States. Similar stories as Maynard's were related: not learning the language and nameless Chinese. This program was made in commemoration of Levaco's father's friend, Sidney Epstein, who was brought up believing that since the Jews were an oppressed people they should not, in turn, oppress anyone else. Epstein stayed on in China through the many ups and downs of that country. My own personal memory in this context is a sign in a park in the old International Settlement of Shanghai that read, "Chinese and dogs not allowed."

Past or present, I have met and known many Westerners who lived in China or made a living as "China experts" but never learned the language. Yet, it is considered reprehensible that anyone should live and work in the United States without learning English. I do think that a unifying language is absolutely essential. What I question is the part that power plays in this debate. Europeans did not make America their home by adopting Native Americans' languages and customs. Is it to be true that if a group has power, be it military, cultural, or economic, then that group can use any language it pleases? What is the nature of this "power" that works like magic, pervasively, in many parts of the world? The military and economic powers of the United States entitle it to the label superpower. Here, I would like to speculate on this source of power from the American lifestyle that can penetrate people's lives without ever showing outward force.

Doi, the Japanese psychiatrist mentioned earlier, recalling his first trip to the United States, notes that he was "dazzled by the material affluence of America and impressed by the cheerful, uninhibited behavior of its people" (1981, p. 11). I recall seeing a cartoon in *The New Yorker* in the 1980s when China had just opened its doors to the West. American cultural ambassadors, McDonald's, and Coca-Cola had since arrived into the welcoming arms of the Chinese. The cartoon depicted mountainous terrain with a long line of the People's Liberation Army stretching over the entire area. The caption read, "Long march goes better with Coca-Cola." Americans, at least from afar, always look as if they are having so much fun, with not a worry in the world. "Have a good time," "Have a great weekend," to paraphrase, are as American as apple pie. The word "have" denotes ownership. To be the owner of good times is magical. In commercials, regardless of what is being sold, the people are shown with broad smiles and bouncy steps; they are articulate, witty, and sexy. The individuals featured in these commercials are becoming increasingly diverse. First came African Americans and, recently, a few Asians. However, they all behave in the same way. Even older Americans have to appear youthful and "fit." How can anyone not envy a lifestyle such as this? These are portraits of winners. Since there is so little substantial interracial and international familiarity, this myth of eternal youth, vitality, and good times can be sustained for a long time.

Fei Xiaotong, regarded as China's most eminent anthropologist and sociologist, after his two-year U.S. visit in 1943 and 1944, remarked that what characterized Americans is boldness:

> To understand America one must look at a youth of sixteen. Every cell in a sixteen-year-old's body is reproducing, growing, and not yet at maturity; but this body can already exist independently. The growth cells are synthesized into a bold and spirited confidence. (Fei, 1979b, p. 173)

However, thirty-five years later, in 1979, Fei made a second visit to the United States. On seeing the wall-to-wall graffiti in New York's subway stations, Fei wrote:

> Graffiti, as I see it, are something like yielding to an irrepressible desire to curse; they are a reaction against the new society symbolized by superhighways and the social polarization that it has brought. Such a feeling cannot be washed clean in the present American social system. (1979a, p. 274)

In regard to the technological advances America has made, Fei observed:

> But the masses of people are coming increasingly to feel that they have fallen unwillingly into a situation where their fate is controlled by others, like a moth in a spider web, unable to struggle free. (1979a, p. 277)

I quote Fei because I think his observations were made from the fresh and keen eye of a professional observer from a distant land. He has described well the two sides of the American individualism coin. Tom Freidman of *The New York Times* reported that, in many parts of the world, "globalization" is seen as "Americanization." There seems to be some truth in this statement. However, I don't think that Americanization is necessarily America's "fault." People all over the world, certainly in China, are only too eager to imitate Americans. This imitation, by definition, is superficial. Only through trained observations and true familiarity can one differentiate substance from appearance. Too many young Chinese Americans, watching from a distance, have been conditioned to assume whatever is Chinese is inferior. That is the basis of their internalized inferiority.

Chapter 4

Emotions: Coping Style, Allocation, and Communication

In previous chapters, I have used events from the 1998 Winter Olympic Games to illustrate certain phenomena. Citing examples that are publicly known is perhaps the most effective way to make cross-cultural comparisons because we can all use the same reference point.

At the 1988 Olympics opening ceremony, American athletes, in their enthusiasm, to the chagrin of their South Korean hosts, became intermingled with other countries' formations while entering the stadium. It was equally noticeable during the medal ceremonies in this and other Olympic meets that the Chinese athletes were as reserved in their display of emotions as the Americans were expansive. In the 1996 Olympics, one of the Chinese gymnasts performed so well that she was a medal hopeful. She remained expressionless while leaving the platform. Unknown to them, the microphone had not been turned off, and when she returned to her team, their screaming and excitement were broadcast for all to hear. The American commentator said, cooly, "The Chinese are celebrating a little too soon." Here we see examples of similar emotions but different choices of where and with whom to express them. To the Chinese athletes, showing pride and joy publicly for personal achievement is unseemly. To Americans, what I achieve is mine to shine, and it is practically unnatural not to do so. Parallel to the Americans' lavish openness and the Chinese restraint, many of the young Chinese Americans I have seen in psychotherapy remarked on their own inabilities to express themselves while "The white people really know how to express their feelings." Often, even when they have made a substantial presentation of a product or project at work, they still feel that they can't "sell" themselves. Again, they experience these occasions not only as a disadvantage but as a sign of their innate inferiority.

I described in Chapter 2 how, in Chinese funerals, signs of sorrow are displayed openly for all to see and hear. In an essay, Roger Rosenblatt praised how, upon returning to work at NBC's *Today Show,* Katie Couric restrained acknowledgment of the death of her husband (Rosenblatt, 1998). This theme is similar to the admiration for Jackie Kennedy's serene poise after President Kennedy was assassinated. At the funeral of China's leader Deng Xiaoping in 1997, his family members wept openly, though quietly, as did President Jiang Zeming. Here, we have a reversal. How shall we understand such opposite behavior in similar circumstances? Obviously, differences exist in when and to whom any of us want to disclose particular aspects of ourselves. To European Americans, happiness from personal achievement is public while grief is more private. In the media, we see reporters going after trauma victims to talk about their emotional sufferings precisely because grief and sorrow are rare "commodities." For the Chinese, it is the reverse. To show joy in one's achievement is self-centered conceit. Grief at a funeral connotes one's affection and loyalty for someone else; it is other-centered.

In this chapter, I will discuss cultural worldviews in relation to commonly used coping styles as well as allocation and communication of emotions. I will also share some of my thoughts and reflections regarding emotions for Chinese Americans, derived from my clinical work.

WORLDVIEWS AND COPING STYLES

At this point, we may do well to recapitulate the basic characteristics of Chinese interdependent and American individualistic cultures in the context of this book is helpful. For the purpose of clarity, I will use simplistic "either-or" demarcations, knowing these traits are points along a continuum and individual differences exist within each culture.

In the Chinese interdependent worldview, the family is the blueprint. One moves outward into the world but always refers back, knowing that family formation is based on mutual support, loyalty, clear hierarchy, emphasis on interpersonal harmony, and delay of one's own personal gratifications. In an individualistic worldview, one is to create one's own destiny, going it alone, and the "I," with its rights and entitlements, is the guiding light. The question is, How do individual persons of one culture differ from those of another in handling emotions in their daily coping behavior?

It may seem far-fetched to refer to ancient Chinese philosophy in a "modern" book such as this. Yet, I am continually amazed at the large repertoire of age-old proverbs and sayings ordinary Chinese, including the illiterate, use as guidelines, justifications, or explanations of actions and opinions. Chinese culture, we note, is the longest uninterrupted one among all the ancient cultures and is still active and influential today. The reservoir of meanings handed down through the millennia is exactly what immigrant parents use to organize their own experiences. Due to both a change in environment and language barriers, these parents experience difficulties in passing on their philosophy of life to their American-reared offspring because counterindications are all around them. Many of the young people in therapy with me referred with disdain and frustration to the "mumbo jumbo" their parents used in lecturing them. The reader is reminded of the many times I have quoted Chinese sayings in this book to explain a Chinese position. These timeless expressions of wisdom do anchor Chinese thinking.

What these immigrant parents want to teach is the paramount importance of "getting along" and delaying one's own individual desires. To achieve interpersonal harmony, one must learn to endure immediate frustration and disappointment for the larger good. The Chinese word for endurance is *ren,* formed by a knife on top of the word for "heart." (More will be said about the heart later in this chapter.) This one powerful word is often depicted on decorative articles on display in gift shops, showing its ever-present application in everyday life. Children are not encouraged to "speak up." Instead, they are told to *ting hua,* literally, listen to the speech/talk/words of elders, implying obedience. These two words illustrate a reliance on traditions passed down from one generation to the next. The virtue of endurance is clearly reflected in Chinese folk tales. Unlike the Western male dragon-slaying aggression motif, Chinese tales employ much slower-paced and unobtrusive means that rely on careful and intelligent observation, planning, and, yes, endurance to achieve the final goal. The protagonist is usually a woman who is chaste, loyal, and smart. Most of the immigrant parents whom I know through their children lived out these qualities to ensure a secure life in a new land to raise their children. From knowing the young people as I do, I would say that the parents did well. The Chinese orientation and approach are the opposite of Western individualistic ways. Imagine what it must be like to live between these two forces!

Another aspect of Chinese coping style is its emphasis on a type of reasoning that would be seen as rationalization in the West. An intriguing practice is *quan* (pronounced "chuan"), which has no English equivalent, reflecting absence of this approach in English-speaking cultures. *Quan* involves reasoning, guidance, consolation, and advice to someone in distress. A few typical lines would be "Don't be so angry; you have to consider your body," meaning anger is bad for one's health; "It's not worth such heartaches"; or advice to *xiang kai dian,* literally, to think a little more widely or openly, similar to saying not to dwell on something or to "let go" of something. The Chinese are fond of saying

dashi   hua   xiaoshi,   xiaoshi   hua   wushi

To melt large conflicts to small ones
and small ones to no conflict.

One may also *quan* a person who is angry, *suanle,* literally, "accounted for," meaning to overlook the "debt" or injustice as if all has been balanced.

The most formal format of conflict resolution is mediation by a third party, usually an older person who is trusted and respected by both sides. This person will talk to the feuding parties separately. Such a structure accomplishes three goals. First, each person has an opportunity to air grievances. Second, direct confrontation and combat are avoided. Third, by honoring and giving face to the mediator, both parties tend to yield some ground toward a resolution. Note here the absence of encouragement to reflect on the event or on one's inner experience of it. In other words, this practice is not intrapsychic and is consistent with the other-directed orientation.

Another perspective that is also consistent with the other-directed orientation is the belief that things will improve only if others change. This hope and pressure for others to change to make life easier for oneself is not uniquely Chinese. Psychotherapists and our own everyday observations of ourselves and others will attest to this statement. The difference is in the intensity of the efforts to control and manipulate others. Such "manipulation" does not have to be devious or bad. It can take the form of being kind, thoughtful, or doing favors to network, to put the other in a better mood and in debt to oneself. To the younger generation who live in a culture in which being "out in the open" and "up front" are sanctioned, this approach is too indirect and seems to them to be dishonest and insincere. The word manipulation has a bad connotation in American society, even though we all use it. The traditional Chinese approach recognizes that much time is needed to cultivate networks that will last a lifetime. In a mobile society such as the United States, we rarely see or need this type of support and relatedness. (For anyone interested in studying this profound and uniquely Chinese cultural behavior, I recommend Mayfair Yang's (1993) book *Gifts, Favors and Banquets: The Art of Social Relationships in China.*)

Finally, I must pay tribute to the overarching Chinese concept of *ming,* usually translated as fate or destiny. Actually the word is anchored in *shengming,* life. I pay tribute to this concept instead of "discussing" it because I do not have the scholarship to "discuss" it. The philosophical, experiential, and spiritual implications in this one word are so profound that one best leave it be! The Chinese use this word frequently, but Westerners dismiss it as "superstition," which is equivalent to "ignorance." Americans, including Chinese Americans, accept terms such as "coincidence" and "synchronicity" as if they explain more than *ming.* In the age of increasing recognition of genetic "predisposition," it is humbling that science and rationality hint but not conclude. Praying to God is "religion," but praying to ancestors is "superstition." Among other conflicting concepts, young Chinese Americans are also caught between these confusing labels. A third-generation Chinese-American woman spent a large sum of money to buy a stone bead to wear around her neck because she was told the bead had been blessed by a Buddhist monk to bring her good health. This woman suffered some serious illnesses and is in a genetic high-risk group for reoccurrence. To me, what she did is not all that different from other means of reaching beyond one's own resources to cosmic power. The Chinese often use *ming* in a summary way to explain or resign themselves to life events, both good and bad. By making it more cosmic, both the pain and the pleasure seem less personal and the experience becomes part of a much larger meaning.

What I wish to point out by mentioning these commonly used Chinese coping styles is that they all lead one's awareness away from one's inner experiences, in meaning or in feeling. As a sharp contrast, an individualistic culture, from which psychotherapy originated and to which it has contributed, values self-awareness, knowing one's "inner voice," "being true to one's self," and being responsible for oneself. Self-expression is highly valued. Verbal skills are traditionally the main vehicle in psychotherapy, as is in social interaction, and let us not forget the talk shows, the more personalized, the better. Getting things "out of one's system" is somehow immediately cleansing and satisfying. "Freedom of speech" is used to justify all kinds of behavior. In short, this voluminous outpouring of words adds to the image of an American "quick fix" culture. This applies to all spheres of life, including relationships and one's emotional state, moving toward an increasingly narcissistic lifestyle. Yet, this very narcissism is also what makes American life appealing to many Chinese and others, as I have mentioned in previous chapters. To actually live in American society having been raised with Chinese coping styles can easily confuse and immobilize the young. Some of them resolve to simply stay with their "own people," even though they live right next to what makes them uncomfortable. The result is a smaller life space and fewer options. Others may go to the other extreme by denouncing their origins and mingling exclusively with white people. This, too, is often unsatisfactory, for sooner or later they realize the fundamental differences and the futility of denial. Still a third option is to enter both worlds. Here, too, conflicts mount in the midst of confusing messages. In my practice I see mostly young people from the second and third groups. This is hardly surprising, since one must have some exposure to Western ways to even consider psychotherapy as an option.

ALLOCATION AND COMMUNICATION
OF EMOTIONS

Apo Hsu, who was appointed conductor and music director of the Bay area Women's Philharmonic Orchestra in 1997, described how her family communicated feelings, not by words, but by gestures, glances, and actions. She grew up in Taiwan, shy and introverted until she learned how to express herself through music. "My family is not very verbal. We don't really say how we really feel, but I can see it in her (mother's) eyes, gestures, her body language—and she doesn't say the words, 'I'm really proud.' I just feel it" (Yip, 1997a, p. 5).

Hsu's experience is representative of what I often hear from Chinese Americans I see in psychotherapy. The topic comes up frequently because of the acute longing and disappointment they feel. They are aching to be understood by their parents and to be told so verbally. They cannot understand why their parents never ask them about their work, interests, feelings, aspirations, as the parents on television shows do or as is suggested in self-help books. Furthermore, in many of their homes, anger is the only emotion that works overtime in their families. Family members yell at one another or resort to silence, sarcasm, and whatever else hurts. The Chinese-American population, aside from the usual neuroticisms from which no country or culture is exempted, must also recall hardships experienced by the parents. Hardships, when overwhelming, have a numbing effect on a person. Most of the young people I worked with came from homes with parents who were truly overworked, tired, weary, and emotionally drained. It is therefore even more remarkable that parental efforts enabled the children to achieve as much as they have. In this sense, these parents have been good role models.

The reader, by now, may be able to supply some conjectures as to the causes of these families' problems. I indicated in the last section how typical Chinese coping styles, by and large, direct awareness away from the individual. I would like now to introduce two other "channels" by which the Chinese communicate their inner experiences. These idioms are rooted in the corporeal body—I shall call them "body-rooted" idioms—and in linguistic capabilities.

Body-Rooted Idioms

I mentioned earlier that I would again address the role of "heart," *xin*, in Chinese language and culture. Even in everyday conversations of the Chinese, one notices how frequently body-related words are used. Heart, or *xin*, dominates this phenomenon. Expressions either employ this word directly or include words that have *xin* as their radical, or the root part, indicating their meaning is in the domain of the heart. In addition to *xin*, I will also discuss *qi* (pronounced chi), essentially life force, energy, breath, air, and *shenti*, body, and their crucial roles in expressing affective meanings for the Chinese. Most of the material is based on my article "Symbolic Meanings of the Body in Chinese Culture and 'Somatization'" (Tung, 1994).

I can think of no better way to introduce *xin* that will also point to a fundamental East-West cultural difference than to begin with the word *xiang*, to think. This character is formed with a heart radical under a word meaning to ponder, to deliberate. In other words, thinking is a joint function of intellect and affect, a type of intuitive synthesis. It is not purely cerebral linear logic. In this one word, the Chinese cut through the body-mind dichotomy so basic to Western thinking. Whether in Chinese philosophy of life, traditional medicine, or everyday behavior, this monolithic "oneness" is assumed. The Chinese do not say "peace of mind."

They say *xin an,* peace of the heart. This cultural difference between Western dichotomy and Chinese or Eastern mono-morphism is the root cause of a great deal of misunderstanding. The West sees the Eastern position as unscientific and ambiguous; the East sees the Western position as mechanical and rigid. Interestingly enough, this very monomorphism shows us how emotions are actually a part of every aspect in Chinese life, when an activity such as thinking is based on the heart. This will become more clear as we examine other body-rooted words.

I have often appreciated the poetic quality in some *xin* idioms. To be discouraged is *hui xin,* meaning the heart has turned to ashes. To relax, to feel at ease, is *fang xin,* to put down/rest one's heart. Mood is *xin jin,* territory of the heart. Sadness is *bei,* formed with the word for negation above a heart radical. Sorrow is *shang xin,* the heart is wounded. To love someone dearly, especially a child, is often expressed by *xin tong,* the heart is aching (over the child). The same term also refers to the bodily sensation, as in chest pain.

In my research project, in explaining what *xin* meant to them, Chinese-speaking informants clearly attributed ethical concerns to the heart. "This word (heart) is the center for the Chinese. If your heart is not good then your entire person is not good," and "To know a person's heart is to know the entire person" (Tung, 1994, p. 486). These informants also referred to kindness, thoughtfulness, mercifulness, and generosity as "good," all in the domain of the heart. In short, "The heart represents the ruler. The heart is everything about you. All your thoughts, emotions, and intelligence belong to the heart" (Ibid.). Note here the personal and interpersonal qualities in morality and ethics for the Chinese, compared to in Christianity where morality is between the individual and God.

The second body-rooted Chinese idiom, *Qi,* has become popular with the increasing attention paid to Eastern healing arts. This is another word that has no English equivalent. It has been translated as life force, energy, breath, air, and, to the initiated, simply *qi*. In relation to emotions, my research informants connected *qi* most frequently with anger. In fact, to be angry is *sheng qi,* literally, birth of *qi*. Intense anger or rage is *qi fen,* depicting hot steam bursting forth. Note here the force and dynamic quality of *qi* in contrast to the calm and still qualities of *xin*. Whereas *xin* is more interpersonal and social, *qi* is related to a person's fate or destiny. *Fu qi* is good, prosperous, and "blessed" *qi; mai qi* is unlucky and unfortunate *qi*. There is nothing the person can do about it. *Qi* is a given. In the context of this book, these meanings also reveal acceptance and resignation, as well as the philosophy of oneness with nature that is the monomorphism position. To challenge *qi* is similar to fighting oneself. So often, when disappointed at something, the Chinese say *meiyou fuqi,* no lucky *qi,* as an explanation. This attitude also makes letting go of the original desire easier.

The third body-rooted word I will discuss is *shenti,* body. Without exception, research informants explained expressions containing *shenti* as being related to the person. Some of them simply substituted "body" in the original text to "the person," "the self," or used a personal pronoun in their responses. The informants spoke of *shenti* as capable of thinking, feeling, and experiencing. The expression *ti hui,* to empathize, was defined by an informant as "When you truly understand and feel for it the body can feel the vibrations so you can understand without words." *Ti yang,* a firsthand experience, is explained as "To truly understand you must experience with your own body," and *shen fen,* literally a portion of the body, or social status, as "The body can feel and sense. This sense tells you of your position in the world" (Tung, 1994, p. 488).

I hope, by these examples, the reader is able to sense a unique quality of Chinese "affective" expressions; they are very different from the direct American expressions of feelings. Chinese terms are often pregnant with connotations and philosophical understanding, and, most of all, are extremely interpersonal.

"Emotion" to the Chinese is not a separate sphere in a dichotomy. One cannot just look at the surface of these words but has to appreciate them against a rich matrix of meanings. Some of the young Chinese Americans I see in my office complain of their parents' or their own "somatic" symptoms as unworthy of attention, as inferior forms of a distress signal. This bias is shared by many mental health professionals and is encouraged by traditional Western psychodynamic psychotherapy in which only inner reflections are "legitimate" concerns.

Earlier, while introducing *xin,* heart, I stated that in the oneness of body and mind, a person's emotions are actually everpresent. This monomorphism is clearly reflected in traditional Chinese medicine (TCM) and is worth mentioning here. A TCM doctor also will frequently *quan* (advise, guide, console) a patient not to worry too much and to learn to *xiang kai dian,* to relax and think more "openly." While in Beijing doing consultation in 1986, I visited a TCM doctor. We had never met before. As soon as I sat down, she said, nonchalantly, "You think a lot. You are too complicated. That's not good for your health. However, you are also straightforward and open (*kailang zhishuai*), so they balance out." I was speechless. Am I not the psychologist?!

Linguistic Capabilities of a Culture

In Chapter 1, I discussed how the degree of refinement in a language reveals cultural values and emphasis. In the Chinese case, for example, familial and relational terms are far more fine-tuned than in English. The same holds true for "rice," the main staple of the Chinese. The word for "rice" is different depending on whether it is in the field, *dao;* unprocessed, *k'o;* processed but uncooked, *mi;* and cooked, *fan.* Compared to English, Chinese does not have a fund of direct and precise words for emotions and affects. In body-rooted idioms, we see examples of rich but hidden meanings that would be considered as "affective" and are used instinctively. Use of metaphors and plays on words that sound the same but have entirely different, sometimes opposite, meanings are abundant in Chinese language. As another example of the Chinese communication style, I will discuss how nature metaphor and symbolism are used for self-expression.

During World War II, there were many dislocated Chinese from Japanese-occupied Eastern China. There were numerous haunting songs to express loneliness and longing for home. Repeatedly, these songs used nature as a metaphor for a range of sentiments and emotions. The moon, the stars, clouds, mountains, rivers, fallen leaves, the seasons richly endowed the lyrics. Sentiments were expressed in images, such as a lone person on an empty beach, watching the waves and the clouds, just to think, "Behind the white clouds is my home." Bright moonlit nights almost always suggested melancholy. Lovers, living at the two ends of the Yangtze River, were depicted as consoled by the thought that they drank water from the same river. Themes of longing for one's elderly parents, family, and home, are brought forth with mountains and rivers as their backdrop. Nature imagery and metaphors are indispensable in classical Chinese poetry. In classical-style landscape paintings, one has to look carefully to find human figures, so tiny and insignificant in contrast to the monumental mountains and the edgeless void.

These art forms do not state the emotions directly. *"Chujing shenging"* is a familiar recitation, meaning one's sentiment is touched off by the scenery. Another familiar sentiment among expatriates originated from the Tan dynasty poet Li Bai:

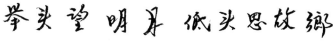

jutou   wang   mingyue,   ditou   si   guxiang

When I looked up and saw the moon, I'd bow
my head in reminiscence of my homeland.

These poetic and eloquent expressions sound clumsy and stilted when translated into English precisely because the cultural context is missing. The Chinese tend to create an ambience, an atmosphere that kindred souls will intuit. These images, passed down through thousands of years, automatically trigger certain sentiments in the Chinese. I recall, in 1993, while teaching in Changsha, Hunan Province, China, one night while on the balcony of my room, I noticed the bright full moon and how beautiful the city looked, and the thought suddenly struck me, "This is the very same moon I have seen for the past forty years in America!" Emotions and thoughts surged. Yes, the Chinese in me is very much alive and emoting.

In contrast, in American English, the word "love" leads in popularity. This word is so much in demand that it has been abbreviated as a heart-shaped symbol for easy transfer to bumper stickers and coffee mugs. The word "great," for enhancement, is a close second to "love." Another interesting aspect of American English is its energetic, swift, no-nonsense expressions, such as the following: someone is a "knockout"; something can "knock your socks off"; going out to "kick some butts"; something demanding is "cutthroat"; making a large profit is "making a killing"; and, of course, "give them hell," etc. Americans know, or "sense," what these expressions mean. They would be meaningless translated into Chinese. Slang reflects local color even more vividly. Even in Chinese slang such action expressions are rare, though one may find a few in martial arts novels. The vast difference between these two linguistic traditions, plus the language barrier, marks the distance between the young Chinese Americans and their immigrant parents. This distance and its effect on parent-child relationships and on Chinese-American self-identity cannot be overstressed. Here, we are literally comparing apples and oranges, without being aware that we are.

On NBC's May 11, 1998, *Today Show,* a child psychologist was asked about ways to help children who hate too much to lose. "Identifying the feelings" was top of the list. In contrast, I saw a thirty-minute television story on "China in Change" (August 24, 1997) about an eleven-year-old boy in Guangxi Province whose parents were killed in an automobile accident en route to register him for a violin competition. Help came from all directions. He was funded to go to several competitions and to continue his violin lessons. No mention was made of his emotional needs separate from his total well-being. By helping the boy with specific needs, the Chinese cared for the entire person. There was no mention of psychotherapy or counseling. The boy already had a big "family" around him. During a ceremony in a large auditorium, he thanked all those who had helped him and addressed them as *ye ye, nai nai, shu shu, ahyi,* or grandpas, grandmas, uncles, and aunts. The English translation was the impersonal "ladies and gentlemen."

In summary, unlike in American English, Chinese language does not have a separate, rich, and pure "category" of words to communicate emotions. Consistent with interdependent boundary and monolithic worldview, Chinese affective expressions are mostly included in body idioms, nature metaphors, concrete actions, ethical codes, and societal expectations. For American-reared Chinese, direct verbal communication is the only type that "counts"; all else is inferior. In my psychotherapeutic work with these Chinese Americans, their desire to "confront" their parents is a frequent topic. Some of them had already tried it, but their American way of communication failed to clarify anything; it only added to the misunderstanding, hurt feelings, and alienation. Others are afraid to try because they do not know how to do it, or they fear their parents' reactions. Still others feel they "should" do it, if only to be "honest," as they have read in books and seen in movies. Our focus becomes knowing what about themselves they want their parents to know and then searching for a more suitable way to achieve that goal. I call the East-West contrast in styles "water versus rock," in that water flows around the rock. Water is discreet and indirect, whereas rocks are obvious and nonyielding.

EMOTIONAL AWARENESS
FOR CHINESE AMERICANS

As we acquire an overview of cultural differences in attitudes and behavior regarding emotionality and self-awareness, two portraits begin to emerge. The portraits will appear different to different viewers depending on which cultural lens the viewer uses. Through the European-American lens, the Chinese may appear passive, reserved, boring, inarticulate, but intelligent, reliable, and hardworking. Through the Chinese lens, European Americans may appear impulsive, superficial, insensitive, self-absorbed, but fun and confident. The two behavior styles are governed by two different sets of rules, although one is not necessarily superior or inferior to the other. Each style has its advantages and drawbacks.

I have pointed out how, in Chinese coping styles, a person's awareness is usually directed away from the person's subjective, personal, inner meanings and reactions. To do otherwise is considered selfish, which in an interdependent context is by far a more serious fault than in an individualistic context. It is like undressing in public! I have repeatedly found confusion in Chinese Americans about the difference between "self-awareness" and "self-indulgence." They mistakenly view paying attention to one's own feelings the same as disregarding others' feelings, a 180-degree reversal from the way they were raised. They consider such behavior as being too "narcissistic."

Another frequent misunderstanding I have noticed is the judgment of "right" or "wrong" feelings. This is a common misunderstanding, not limited to Chinese Americans. Here, feelings are confused with actions. This judgment often results in not facing up to one's "unacceptable" feelings. The clarification they often need is that we are not "responsible" for our feelings, but we are responsible for our actions. The compass is a good analogy in this case. The compass, like our feelings and reactions, gives us the information, but the person decides which direction to take. The person is then responsible for the decision and the action. That with self-awareness comes responsibility is a new concept for them. In psychotherapy with Chinese Americans, this "awareness" cannot stop at just one's own internal representations and experiences, or intrapsychic meanings. It must also be heavily interpsychic, to include essential others such as parents and their experiences and realities. Many times the young Chinese Americans I worked with told me that cultural and historical knowledge helped them in resolving difficulties with their parents and relatives. Prior to this they looked at the older generation, as well as themselves, through the European-American lens and came away feeling inferior and discouraged. The responsibility that comes with new knowledge challenges them. Gradually, they become more creative and "culturally sensitive" in their methods of conflict resolution with their families and with "Americans," as well as in their self-understanding. The opposite of "passivity" is not necessarily aggression or even assertiveness. It is, first of all, clarity. "Clarity" for Chinese Americans includes knowing one's own "irrational" aspects (feelings, dreams, fantasies, wishes, and desires) and cultural origins of behavior, both East and West. This is more work for a bicultural person, but it is also potentially richer.

I have three main reasons why I believe that emotional awareness is important to, and attainable for, Chinese Americans.

My first concern is, since they live in an environment with core values and behaviors that emphasize personal feelings and the "self," it is too bewildering not to be familiar with that worldview. One needs a "bridge," a sense of continuity, to one's environment to reduce fragmentation. In the previous chapters, I mentioned how some of the young Chinese-American professionals I worked with had expressed their envy and admiration for Caucasian Americans' abilities to express themselves. Clear articulation requires knowing both the issues being discussed and one's own stand on them. The latter necessitates self-awareness, an ability to look inward and to move away from the "I don't know how I feel" state. Positioned at a vista point to see both Eastern and Western behavior patterns, Chinese Americans have the unique potential to develop a more integrated understanding of life. In fact, the "trend" toward a higher level of integration is now very much in the American consciousness, combining East and West in medicine, religion, and worldview.

A second reason is the increased research in recent years showing the connection between the body and the mind in one's total well-being. The foundation of emotions lies in the corporeal body. The so-called "somatic" symptoms are often signals of "blockage" in the process of living. These body-mind research findings are coming closer to the Chinese monolithic oneness philosophy discussed earlier. For a people rich in body-related experiences, being more conscious of the clues from the body can only be beneficial to self-understanding.

The third and, to me, most significant reason is that emotional awareness teaches the person that he or she is not always the victim. It allows for creativity. Let me explain.

Some years ago, a friend called to consult about a Chinese neighbor who was crying and screaming, getting "hysterical" on the street because of some in-law problems. When I worked at psychiatric clinics, a number of incidents involved Chinese patients who were said to be running and screaming on the streets until police took them to a psychiatric treatment setting. A Chinese term, *majie,* means, literally, street scolding. The expression calls to mind an image of, usually, a woman, who is the least powerful in Chinese society, standing on a street, yelling and cursing, at no one in particular, at least not by name. The guilty party and others know at whom the public display is aimed. By going public as a last resort, she ensures the opponent will at least lose face, without having a direct confrontation. Injustice is voiced, and, hopefully, group pressure or a family mediator will bring about some change. Indirect approaches such as *majie* or becoming physically ill can be powerful. They do sometimes bring about situational changes. However, they always require a prolonged period of suffering to "justify" the dramatic display and ill health used to gain sympathy. The pivotal cross-cultural point is that the "messages" communicated by this type of behavior will be lost or misunderstood in American society. The behavior will most likely be interpreted as the person is "hysterical," "manipulative," "somatizing," or has "lost control." People's reactions will be based on their interpretations, such as by enlisting medical or psychiatric intervention. What is missing in the behavior is the awareness that can be the basis for earlier, self-initiated changes. When there is clarity about what a situation means to us it relaxes its grip on us. The understanding can put some distance between us and the problematic situation to allow for a chance to take appropriate actions, and thus feel less victimized. A sense of helplessness can be, by far, more debilitating than taking a feared action. I realize, of course, that what I have described here can be difficult to achieve and requires time and hard work. At the same time, it can also be liberating to gain a "skill" that is truly one's own.

A final point I would like to make in regard to this theme is more general. It is my belief that when one experiences oneself as a thinking and feeling being, one is more likely to experience other beings, human and animal, as conscious and feeling. This communality is the basis for empathy. Such empathic communality has far-reaching implications in a society as diverse as the United States. In a larger sense, empathy is the foundation for human rights, animal rights, and the quality of our total ecology.

Chapter 5

Moving Out from the Shadow of the Eclipse: Integration

An interesting recent development in my practice has been the arrival of young, college-educated Asians. Some of them had been working with Caucasian therapists but decided that their cultural background is important and wanted to see an Asian therapist. A brief summary of my experiences with this phenomenon can be used as a point of departure.

In the first twelve years of my professional life I treated Caucasian Americans almost exclusively because of the geographic regions in which I lived. When I returned to San Francisco in the late 1970s, I worked with a more diverse population, but still largely Caucasian Americans. The pattern continued into the 1980s, with a few more Asian Americans and occasionally Latino and African Americans. Psychotherapy, to this day, is still largely utilized by persons of European background. The clearest shift, I noticed, began in the early 1990s. At the current time, a majority of the persons I work with are of Asian background, especially second-generation Chinese Americans and Chinese who came to this country at a young age. There seems to be a few major differences between the Chinese Americans whom I saw in the 1970s and 1980s and those in the 1990s. The former group, as a whole, is older, with most people in their forties. Most of them came into treatment complaining of somatic symptoms for which physicians could find no organic basis. Occupationally, they were more likely to have worked either for family businesses or for family friends. Depression, marital problems, and family responsibilities were the central problem areas. The 1990s group, on the other hand, consists mostly of persons in their twenties and thirties with at least a college degree. They are self-referred. Even though they do complain of depression and anxiety, their areas of concern are broader. Self-identity, particularly in the mixed cultural context, their place in society, as well as family and relationship problems are usually the central areas for therapeutic work. As most of them have occupations that require a postgraduate degree, these young people are also concerned about their professional goals and meaningfulness. To some of them, the decision to see an Asian therapist was made with mixed feelings and even apprehension. They wondered if I held the same values as their parents, and would therefore judge and criticize them as their families and relatives do. It is important to them that I have "made it" in mainstream society without being a "banana," which is yellow on the outside and white on the inside. In other words, they want me to be knowledgeable and experienced in "American life" but not by "selling out." Some are concerned whether they can discuss sexual matters with me freely, a topic not discussed in Chinese families. One young woman actually asked if she should talk about her "problems" with me, but "sex" with someone else.

This change is a far cry from the internalized inferiority of earlier years, when a Chinese psychotherapist was automatically assumed to be inferior, when the wish to be "like everybody else," meaning to be like the white people, dominated. Out of shame, embarrassment, and fear, some of them expressed a pronounced wish to hide or deny their ethnic and cultural background. For these same reasons, they have felt uncomfortable or humiliated in telling a Caucasian therapist about parts of their lives that may be "too Chinese." At the same time, they do not want to betray their own family background by bad-mouthing it and subjecting it to further ridicule. "Besides," I would hear, "I am tired of having to explain everything. I don't understand them myself." A few of them have told me that seeing a Chinese therapist makes it harder for them to hide behind a blanket explanation of "That's the Chinese way." The discomfort and inferiority feelings of being a Chinese American are still very much in operation today. Some still believe a white therapist can better teach them about the "American way." A century-old wound requires more time and corrective experiences for healthy new growth to take place. What I do see is evidence of a process toward better integration. Strictly speaking, this is but a continuation of the self-identity process. Multiple and interrelated factors from both America and China continue to contribute to this new phase as well.

IN AMERICA

The Coming of Age of Second-Generation Chinese Americans

Throughout the book I have cited personal experiences of Chinese Americans who are now nationally known. Their growing-up experiences closely resemble what I hear from those who consult with me. With different levels of integration and cohesion, these young people are struggling to emerge from the darkness behind an eclipse to a place in the sun, to be truly on par with "everybody else." Their generation is better educated, has had wider social exposure and more opportunities, and has more self-awareness than their immigrant parents.

In the past two decades, an increasing number of achievements have had Chinese names and faces attached to them. Whether literature, music, architecture, academics, Nobel Prize laureates, politics, etc., the pioneers have been eye-catching. A couple of recent examples will illustrate. After the 1998 Winter Olympics, when Michelle Kwan was mentioned in one media coverage as though she was not an American, the Chinese-American skater starred in Disney's *Reflections on Ice,* in the part of Mulan, which was aired on ABC on June 10, 1998. Along with her were skaters of all colors, skating the parts of Chinese and Hun soldiers. It was a delight to behold. During the months of Bill Lann Lee's nomination procedure for the position of Assistant Attorney General, Civil Rights Division, a Chinese American, for the first time in U.S. history, was thrust into the center of a heated debate of this nature. As the number of such events increases, our society will become "desensitized" in the process. Seeing a Chinese or Asian face will no longer be unusual.

These achievements and visibility, I believe, contributed greatly to the aspirations and comfort levels of young Asian and Chinese Americans in general. Gradually, they are becoming more adventuresome and investigating more possibilities. A *Los Angeles Times* feature article, "The Changing Face of Higher Education" (Hong, 1998), confirmed this perception, when it reported that one in four undergraduates at Stanford and Wellesley are Asian Americans. Other major universities, such as Harvard, New York, and Northwestern, report that about 20 percent of their undergraduates are of Asian-American background. In the University of California system, the figures are most impressive: Asian Americans represent 40 percent at Berkeley and 58 percent on the Los Angeles campus. Even though biology and electric engineering remain the most popular majors, an increasing number of young Asian Americans are going into business, English, and history, and they are more visible in other aspects of campus life than ever before. Some scholars even predict that this generation of Asian-American students could become the next minority group to profoundly shape American intellectual life, as did Jewish college students in the first half of this century. I hasten to add, however, that this encouraging new wave of achievement involves only a minority among Chinese and other Asian Americans. I have often heard cautionary remarks that the label "model minority" is a mixed blessing. It inspires respect as well as conceals existing problems such as underachievement, unrealistic expectations, and insufficient attention and help given to those who are not in the "cream of the crop" group. Besides, such a label can easily create an expectation that causes any departure to be greeted with suspicion and rejection. I am keenly aware that the population I work with belongs to the "elite," but none of them was born with a silver spoon. Through painstaking efforts and sacrifices on their and their parents' parts, they have achieved thus far. I cannot recall a single exception to this pattern.

In his statement at the Senate Judiciary Committee hearing, Bill Lann Lee told of his father's patriotism and esteem for the United States. The senior Mr. Lee volunteered for the Army Air Force during World War II, fought in the Pacific, and achieved the rank of corporal. While in the army he was called a "dumb Chinaman" because of the way he looked and spoke. Yet, Mr. Lee told his two sons that he was treated "like everyone else." After the war ended, he could not find an apartment even when wearing his uniform. "He found there were no job opportunities for a Chinese-American veteran in post-war America, so he took off his uniform and went back to the laundry." The young attorney general designate went on to say of his father, "He could not escape a world of bias, but America afforded his children opportunities that my brother and I would not have had anywhere else" (Lee, 1997, p. 9).

To be able to emerge from the darkness with their faith and aspirations intact, the Lee father and son demonstrate the best of this dynamic integrative process.

Made in China

A shift of paramount importance to the process of integration of Chinese Americans was political in nature. It occurred officially on January 1, 1979, when the United States of America and the People's Republic of China normalized their relationship after thirty hostile years. Major political changes are always followed by slower social changes. Changes on the level of people's everyday lives are usually gradual and spontaneous.

I recall in the 1950s, when I was a new immigrant, I joked about how, in San Francisco's Chinatown, only the people were "made in China." All the goods in the shops seemed to be "made in Japan." Up until President Nixon's 1972 visit to China, the only place one could find Chinese food in San Francisco was Chinatown. The restaurants served mostly the southern, Cantonese cuisine. Gradually, in the 1970s, Chinese restaurants began to branch out. Consumers' demands also became more sophisticated and varied. I remember the first time, in Berkeley, California, my family had *shaobing,* a type of flat bread from northern China; we thought it was heavenly. Our excitement was not due to only the taste of this very ordinary food; our emotions came from the combination of a touch of something so familiar and the new reality that a glimpse of "home" was on the horizon. In fact, the few *shaobings* we had were burned on the outside and slightly raw on the inside, but these imperfections were accepted with good-natured humor.

Now, Chinese restaurants are numerous in large American cities and available throughout the country. In cities such as San Francisco, one can choose foods from all parts of China, for breakfast, lunch, dinner, and late-night snacks. Also, one sees practically everybody in these restaurants, Chinese or not, using chopsticks. Grocery stores are selling all types of Chinese and other Asian foods, and businesses are booming. Young people and newcomers from China take this scene for granted. Only in retrospect can one appreciate the changes.

Another major "import" from China since the late 1980s is Chinese movies. The earlier ones, such as *Red Sorghum* (1987), made a deep impression on American audiences. Most Americans, including Chinese Americans, had never been exposed to Chinese films before. Within a short period of time, quality movies, such as *Raise the Red Lantern* (1991), *Qui Ju* (1992), *Farewell My Concubine* (1993), and *Red Firecrackers, Green Firecrackers* (1994), from China, and *Wedding Banquet* (1993) and *Eat, Drink, Men and Women* (1994), from Taiwan, were being offered. These movies made at least three contributions to the theme of the social atmosphere for Chinese Americans' self-identity. The first one is the world-class artistry these films demonstrated. Several of them won prestigious awards in Europe. Second, the characters in these movies, unlike the plastic imitations conjured up by Hollywood, were real. Through these realistic portrayals, the characters, like real persons anywhere, became flesh and blood individuals one could identify with. Third, these were outspoken films about some ugly and inhuman aspects of Chinese traditions and social realities. But because of their superb artistry and realistic characterizations, they promoted understanding and respect from Western audiences instead of defaming China or the Chinese. After all, audiences usually respond to the souls of individual characters when they are well presented and do not see the stories as one-dimensional, isolated samples of what China is. In other words, these movies opened up what many Chinese Americans were too ashamed or ignorant to reveal. Along with Chinese-American novels, plays, and movies, they helped the Chinese to emerge from their mute shadow. Their worst fear of being looked down upon did not happen. Rather, because of the new openness, Chinese are now taken more seriously than ever before.

As a display of some of China's best, we can also mention Shanghai Tang, an exclusive fashion center opened on November 21, 1997, on New York's Madison Avenue. The store features Mao jackets, the traditional Chinese *gibao* (long, straight dress with a high collar), and fancy Chinese-inspired outfits of quality Chinese fabrics. These garments are marked "Made by Chinese" instead of "Made in China" to distinguish them from the usual products associated with the mediocrity of the more familiar label. To have Chinese-style fashion displayed on Madison Avenue is a first.

Disney's 1998 animated movie *Mulan* is perhaps the best-publicized China-based popular entertainment. It is noteworthy that the voice of the animated main character, Mulan, was that of the Chinese-American actress Ming-Na Wen of *The Joy Luck Club* (1994) and *Golden Child* (1997) onstage. This again is a giant leap forward from the days when Chinese parts were played by Caucasian actors with tortured facial distortions.

Chinese martial arts and other health-oriented skills, such as *qi king* and *taijiquan,* along with traditional Chinese medicine, are making bold entrances in American life. Ch'an Buddhism (more popularly known in America as Zen, the Japanese term) is another major "import" with which Americans of all backgrounds are becoming intrigued. According to a National Public Radio program, *Buddhism in America,* America now has more Buddhists than Episcopalians and the U.S. Army is hiring Buddhist ministers as chaplains.

It is now easier, even though there is still a long way to go, for young Chinese Americans to be themselves. A report in *Asian Week* (Panesar, 1998) described the lighthearted event of the seventh Mr. Asian Northern California contest. A mostly female crowd "whistled and heckled" as the young men went through routines that included tap dance, rifle drill, and push-ups. This type of public display would be unthinkable in their parents' time. It would be great fun to hear from these young men's elders! Perhaps, in the near future, their competition routine will include a demonstration of Eastern martial arts and dance. Likewise, an increasing number of television reporters are now Asians, especially Asian women. The San Francisco Chinese New Year's parade improves each year, embracing participants of all ethnicities in a grand, joyful celebration for the entire community. This annual "ritual" has not always been as successful. We may have a few persistent Chinese Americans who are proud of their heritage to thank for its current success.

Such new phenomena can also be seen as a process of "normalization." They involve a constant exchange between individuals of a subgroup and the larger society. The more we try to hide something, the more "abnormal" this something will feel to us and to others. While growing up, Asian Americans received too many messages from all sides, telling them they were inferior and unacceptable simply because they were different. It takes courage to be visible, to risk sticking out like a sore thumb. The young people I see have often related to me how uncomfortable they feel at events when they are the only Asians. To be conspicuous makes them feel even more self-conscious of being seen as stereotypes, silent and passive.

Paradoxically, viewing integration as a continuation of the self-identity process allows us to examine how "stereotyping" works. Similar to air pollution and water contamination, the most toxic power of stereotyping is that it operates in silence, through the unconscious. Archie Bunker, a character in the television show *All in the Family,* was not dangerous because he was loud and straightforward. Direct and open discrimination can be spotted and dealt with more readily. The term "glass ceiling" points out the invisibility of an institutional barrier. The counterpart of "glass ceiling" is everywhere in our personal lives as well. The harmful effect of stereotyping, in terms of both internalized inferiority and short-changing one's own cultural roots, takes place without the person's awareness. Members of minority groups acquire the attitudes and values of the majority society, as though these positions were "facts" and "reality," and automatically use them as benchmark criteria. It is impossible to guard against something that is all-pervasive. Furthermore, as sociologists remind us, some truth always lies in the stereotypes. The crucial point is to differentiate on an individual basis. Members of both the majority and minority groups have to be on the alert not to make arbitrary assumptions about one another. This is a challenging task indeed. Raised consciousness may help us to see our invisible barriers. The self-examination involved in the search for one's identity as a minority can be a painful and anxiety-provoking experience that most people would rather not enter into. The resistance is understandable. However, I do see more of the young people engaged in determined challenges of these negative images, singly or in groups. Throughout the United States, protests, rallies, and letter writings address unjust and unfair treatment of Chinese and other minority Americans.

IN CHINA

A Positive Mirror Image from the Ancestral Land

In describing the process of self-identity, I used mirror reflection as a metaphor to show that how we see ourselves is fundamentally dependent on how others see us. That the Chinese came to the United States because of deficiencies in their own country is a historical fact. To escape hardship of some kind is a major reason for emigration worldwide. How an individual person is received abroad is very much tied to how the person's place of origin is perceived. All of us have "selves" that are identified by affiliations—family, profession, country, and even residential location—that say something about us. The energetic chanting of "U.S.A." at the Olympic games is an example. This is the "affiliated self."

In *Unbound Feet* (Yung, 1995), the author describes how, in China, when the Republic of China displaced the Qing Dynasty in 1912, Chinese women began to unbind their feet as part of their efforts toward equality. In America, Chinese-American women followed the example of women in China and stopped binding their own and their daughters' feet. The revolution in China served as the impetus for both Chinese and Chinese-

American women to come forth and assert themselves. This nationalistic-affiliated self gained further momentum when Japan invaded China in 1937. Chinese-American women and men saw significance for themselves in the strengthening of China:

> At issue were blood ties and Chinese nationalism, as well as the belief that only through a stronger China could they hope to improve their status in America, where they were treated as unwanted aliens. (Yung, 1995, p. 226)

These transformations, inspired and energized by events in China, showed China to be a country with fighting spirit. Chinese Americans also stepped forth as people with character who can be proactive and self-respecting.

This phenomenon is termed the "group self" in self-psychology, meaning that a nation's people can be either inspired or demoralized, for example, by the quality of the leadership. The nation can be the object of one's love and devotion. Groups can be as vulnerable or courageous as individuals.

From the days when Chinese first arrived in America, China has continuously been in a vulnerable and disturbed state. Second-generation Chinese Americans and their immigrant parents basically had to rely on their own merits and efforts, with little help from their *zuguo,* ancestral land, until the 1980s.

I recall the surreal sensation when I saw the national flag of the People's Republic of China shown for the first time in the United States during Deng Xiaoping's visit in 1979. I experienced a mixture of excitement and disbelief. The same flag had been condemned and outlawed for so many years in America. Suddenly, it was center stage, alongside the American flag. Later, at a soccer game between the China and U.S. teams, both Chinese and American national anthems were played. Then I heard the Chinese spectators in the crowd screaming *"Jia you!,"* "More fuel!" These were sounds from long ago, sounds that I had forgotten.

I also recall, sometime in the 1980s, watching a Bob Hope special from China. I wondered if it would be another show in which, even though produced in China, the Chinese were subordinate and appeared ridiculous. I was pleasantly surprised that performers of both countries shared the limelight. Chinese officials reportedly worked closely with the Americans for this special, and the results were successful. The documentary *From Mao to Mozart* chronicled violinist Isaac Stern's 1979 visit to China. The energy he put forth for the young Chinese music students and audiences spoke for his sincerity. His insistence on high standards, I felt, was precisely because of his respect for the Chinese.

Internationally, China's artistic talents, such as the movies mentioned earlier, also were a strong presence in Europe. In 1995, Italy's Florence Opera House asked Zhang Yimou, the director of *Red Sorghum* and *Raise the Red Lantern,* to stage Puccini's opera *Turandot,* about a mythical princess of ancient China. After some hesitation on Zhang's part, and persuasion on the Florentines' part, the collaboration was successfully presented in Florence in August 1997, with eleven sold-out performances. A year later, as agreed, on September 5, 1998, this same opera played at Beijing's Forbidden City, which is what Puccini imagined for his princess. The princess has come home. *The New York Times* (Eckholm, 1998) compared the grand scale of this production with a "spectacle worthy of Cecil B. DeMille" and a "lavish event staged for the world." Singers and musicians were from Italy. The conductor, as in Florence, was Zubin Mehta. The cast included hundreds of Chinese extras and dancers "that will approach 1,000 members in the grand finale." Eight performances were scheduled; visitors from all over the world were expected. Following this historical endeavor, the Florence Opera House performed Verdi's *Aida* at the inaugural season of the new Shanghai Opera House. This is perhaps the prelude to the emergence of Chinese talents on the world scene.

By far the most significant "joint appearance" took place during President Clinton's state visit to China in June 1998. The historical televised news conference with the two presidents, each representing and speaking for his country, showed equality and mutual respect while addressing substantive and controversial topics. Even American media, for once, were excited and complimentary about the event. At President Clinton's appearance at Beijing University and during his radio call-in in Shanghai, Chinese students and Shanghai residents asked confrontational questions of the American president. Such a boldfaced encounter in China was a new experience for both sides.

Prior to the Clinton China visit, Chinese President Jiang Zemin made his state visit to the United States, in October 1997. In a speech at Harvard University, Jiang reminded us that "[t]he frequent bulling and humiliation by imperialist powers once weakened China [but] China has stood up again as a giant." He also made it clear that China "will proceed from our own national conditions . . . without blindly copying other countries' models" (Editorial, 1997, p. 4). In the television discussions of China's specialists during Jiang's visit, China was referred to as a "major power" or even an up-and-coming "superpower." To hear these labels being applied to China was mind-boggling. What happened to the *"dongya bingfu,"* East Asian weakling, a term patriotic Chinese intellectuals used, in their despair, in confronting their own countrymen earlier in this century? What happened to the China where, as Schneiter (1992) reminds us, not too long ago, "Christianity arrived riding on cannon balls," and problems in foreign policy with China "could be resolved by giving the Chinese an occasional sniff of gunpowder"? (p. 173).

The field of intercultural communication based largely on experiences in international trading has produced a body of literature related to our topic. Similar to Schneiter, these "China hands" try to remind Americans that China is an independent culture with her own history that is to be understood and not remade in the image of America. Books by Edward Hall (1983) and Randall Stross (1990), for those who may be interested, are examples of scholarly intercultural works applied to businesses and government. Hall's works are not specifically about China, but the insights are applicable. Humor seems to be a unique quality in all good intercultural works, as a reliable indicator that the writer or speaker has learned the lesson well and learned it the hard way. How often do we see politicians with such wise humor?

China is still problem-laden and will be so for sometime to come. This fact is an accumulative result of centuries of corruption, political mistakes, and the spinelessness of rulers who periodically ceded China's sovereignty to foreigners to protect their own interests. This shift of one's ancestral land toward becoming more self-respecting perhaps means more to the parents' generation than to the young Chinese Americans. The parents have memories. However, in the context of the total environment in which Chinese Americans' self-identities are formed, these changes are as fundamental as the soil from which plants grow. The degree of meaningfulness varies from person to person. Even though experienced as indirect and secondary by some, it is still significant to the younger generation. They see now that the ancestral land is demonstrating capacities to stand up and speak up and to be on equal footing in dignity with the Western powers. For once, China is not afraid to be a "big tree that will catch much wind" or to "thrust out one's head to show one's face." These are the very qualities the young missed seeing in their parents and in themselves.

"Home" Is an Elusive Word

Speaking of circumstances in China brings us closer to the parents' experiences. I have discussed their initial cultural shock, subsequent alienation, helplessness, and anxiety as a result of their immigration. Many of them are alienated even from their own children. The reaccessibility of their homeland, however, is far from simply being able to "go home" again, literally or psychologically. When E.T. "phoned" and returned home he was only away for a short time. Even in this brief period, he formed attachments with earthlings that influenced his homecoming. The meaning of "home" to those who have been away most of their lives is never simple.

Based on informal observations and subjective impressions, it seems to me that Chinese immigrants in America have gone through three stages since 1979, when normalization of relations between the two countries took place. The first stage was characterized by excitement and heightened emotions. Contacts with "home" and kinfolk were established, with a great deal of goodwill toward one another.

The second stage was marked by a wide range of complex and contradictory emotions on both sides. When memories and life encounters are as different as those for the Chinese who lived on two sides of the Pacific, they leave a huge space for unrealistic assumptions and expectations. The consequences are often disappointment, hurt feelings, resentment, and mutual distrust. Many young Chinese Americans went to China alone or with their parents to meet, for the first time, grandparents, uncles, aunts, and cousins. Most of them were unable to communicate with persons of the parents' past due to the language barrier. Some of them returned from this experience feeling elated for having touched their roots. Others were indifferent. Still others were turned off by their relatives and "their ways" in China. Immigration efforts to bring family members to this country increased. Of these reunions, I have heard tales of actual or suspected betrayal, mistreatment, and bitterness from both sides. At the same time, I have also heard numerous stories of genuine heartwarming reunions. This second stage seemed to be most pronounced in the 1980s.

Two middle-aged brothers and their wives were "sponsored" to come to the United States in the 1980s by a third brother who had been here for many years. The four newcomers were met at the airport by the brother. He brought them home and gave them an afternoon snack. Then they were led to a room in the basement to settle in. Evening came and there was no sign of dinner. They were hungry, tired, and anxious. Eventually, the older brother went upstairs to inquire about food. There, he realized, how unhappy the sister-in-law was about suddenly being responsible for four strangers. They were given some cookies for the night. The newcomers, as did many others in similar or worse circumstances, were able to find odd jobs to support themselves. Seven years later, they have all become U.S. citizens without ever burdening anyone. A young woman physician in her early thirties told me of how badly her own sister, who sponsored her and another sister to come here, treated her. "She treats us like servants because she feels we owe her something." They cleaned house, cooked, and worked for this sister without pay. The idea of entitlement seemed to be operating on both sides. The ones who were left in China and have suffered felt their suffering entitled them to "compensations." Those on the American side feel just bringing them over is "favor" enough. The impressive aspect is the continuation of cordial relationships, at least outwardly. In time, this cordiality was able to recondition their feelings and provide time for mutual understanding. I have also heard from the Chinese-American young adults in therapy with me of sudden appearances of strangers who are "family." Again, reactions toward these new additions varied. They ranged from fascinated curiosity to sympathy, puzzlement, and annoyance. Some of them were eager to show the relatives around and to make them feel welcome. Others saw them as their parents' "problems." It was quite moving to hear how language barriers were overcome through empathy, humor, and fun activities. Here, the word "family" is reason enough.

The third stage, overlapping with the later phase of the second stage, can be described as a movement toward stability. As relatives from the two shores became better acquainted with one another, misunderstanding began to decrease. This stage is gradual, through repeated exposures to and contacts with one another. This stage requires patience and commitment and calls on the goodwill and caring that are rooted in the traditional Chinese values of family and kinship. The branch of the family in China is now mentioned in a more matter-of-fact fashion, as if the novelty and awkwardness have been ironed out.

Visits "home" after a long absence usually involve a peculiar combination of feeling, both familiar and strange. For those who traveled back to China, the desire to "go home," meaning their American homes, is a frequent reaction while in China. They miss the familiarity of their daily lives. The disorientation can be difficult to handle. Once "home" in America, part of oneself seemed to have been left in China. And on it goes. The emotional depth and complexity of immigrant psychology throughout the world concerning where "home" is warrants a book of its own. How these experiences and emotions of the parents are transmitted to their American-born children are little understood. What it means to the parents when their American-born children "go home" to the land of their own childhood is another unexplored experience.

Chapter 6

Ancestral Ghosts Meet Superman:
A New Cycle of Chinese Immigrants

. . . [American's] regard for tradition is to a greater or lesser extent conscious, intellectual, and artificial. It is not the same as ours [Chinese's]. The reason I feel this way is that I have found Americans do not have ghosts. . . . Life in its creativity . . . melds past, present, and future into one inextinguishable, multilayered scene, a three-dimensional body. This is what ghosts are. . . . American children hear no stories about ghosts. They spend a dime at the "drugstore" to buy a "superman" comic book. . . . Superman is not a ghost. Superman represents actual capabilities or future potential, while ghosts symbolize belief in and reverence for the accumulated past. (Fei, 1979b, pp. 177-179)

I quote the above passage because of its beauty and profound insight—to use something I feel is special at the end of this book is like giving a gift to the reader for keeping me company for so long. I hope you have savored it as much as I did.

In this book, I have reached beyond this century into the last century in describing how Chinese first came to America. Being from an old culture, immigrant parents are familiar with ghosts. Their children did not want to hear the stories about ghosts. To them, ghosts are just scary superstitions and nothing else. The elders whisper to their ghosts.

Now, at the threshold of a new century, I am beginning to see another cycle of immigrants from China in my practice, as well as meeting them in the community. Many of these newcomers were professionals in China: physicians, engineers, teachers. Because of the language barrier, they now work as busboys in restaurants, janitors, housekeepers, laborers, and low-level office workers, anywhere they can find a job. These are usually middle-aged men and women who survived the many political "movements" in China and learned the meaning of fear. Some of the young, college-aged students fared better, but they certainly did not have it easy either. As I listen and observe, I find both similarities and differences between these newcomers and the immigrant parents I have written about in this book.

These newcomers are encountering a different experience in America from the one of earlier immigrants. Now, many of them go to community colleges for classes in English as a second language. Their basic civil rights are much better protected, and they are free to travel in this country. Unlike their forerunners, they can now write, phone, and visit back and forth with family members in China. Not surprisingly, however, the psychological similarity of being immigrants is still great and, to a large extent, is cultural in nature. The middle-aged former professionals' main purpose of *chiku,* literally, to eat bitterness, or to endure hardship, is so that their children may have a better life. Even though living conditions back home in China have greatly improved during the past twenty years, they still prefer to stay in the United States for their children's futures. The position of sacrificing for one's offspring is unchanged from the last century. Likewise, the children who came here at a young age show the same pattern of cultural intergenerational conflicts with their parents as was the case in earlier immigrant families. As one of them said, "I wish they didn't make sacrifices for me. Who asked them to? I don't want to listen to it every time I do something they don't like." Socially, these new immigrant parents and older children also keep to themselves, living in close proximity with kinfolk or acquaintances in often crowded areas.

Referrals to me fall mainly into two categories. Many are for situational problems such as conflicts with co-workers. I have repeatedly found circumstantial and cultural misunderstandings in these cases. For example, in their level of employment, they usually work with other ethnic minority immigrants who are also hampered by language deficiency, economic pressure, and a spectrum of psychosocial stresses common to new immigrants. Turf tension can be expected when all groups are loyal to their own and vigilant for better opportunities. When there is conflict, the immediate response on all sides is defensiveness and hostility. Their interpretations of the situations and solutions are, of course, highly conditioned by their respective past experiences. In listening to their stories, I am, once more, impressed by their resilience, endurance, and tough-mindedness. They are not to be deterred. I believe that they have been conditioned by their past experiences in China, that "When the going gets tough, the tough get going." It is a matter of survival of the fittest. One should hold one's ground.

This group of people would stop coming in after the sessions authorized by their Employee's Assistance Program. This is to be expected, both for financial reasons and because psychotherapy and counseling are too alien to them. In the other-directed culture of the Chinese, people seek ways to get out of situational problems. Self-understanding or "growth" are not culturally necessary. Among the ones I have worked with, most acknowledged that having talked about the problems helped them to feel better; it softened their sense of isolation; and it helped them to see the issues more clearly, which led to better solutions. A few actually realized some of their own basic personality patterns that got them in trouble here and back home in China. They often expressed the wish to become friends with me, which, among Chinese, is a great compliment. It meant they felt they could talk to me and trust me. In China, to be socially connected to a doctor is common. To the Chinese, "trust" is synonymous with "friendship" and mutually exclusive with an "outsider" or a "stranger." In the United States, socializing with a patient is considered a "dual relationship" and is frowned upon as being "unethical." This is another reflection of cultural differences in boundary lines.

The second common theme for referrals to me is more personal, namely, marital dissolutions. I have seen several women in their thirties and forties with marital complications who came from large cities such as Shanghai, Beijing, and Guangzhou. Hearing their experiences, I cannot help but think that their stories are by-products of the times. As Qian (1996) described in his book on the current wave of Chinese students in America, growing up in constant political "struggles" that had all but destroyed old traditions, these students are extraordinarily determined, aggressive, and ambitious in what they aim to accomplish. These women also impressed me in this way. In the large Chinese commercial centers, people jostle for positions that will toss them into the whirlwind of opportunities to "get ahead." To them, coming to the United States is like winning the lottery. These jostlings can be ruthless, disregarding personal feelings, loyalty, or even safety. What they thought life in America would be like had little to do with reality. Instead, rumors, hearsay, and wishful thinking constituted their "preparation" for coming to this country. These women have often married to expedite either their own or their spouses' opportunities to come to this country. Keeping in mind that marriage in Chinese life is more a pragmatic responsibility than romance or personal realization, a union for a specific purpose is not that out of place. Or, once here, fighting to realize their dreams, loneliness compelled them into compromising marriages. By the time they came in to see me they were in shock: What happened?! These women reminded me of the old-time "woman warriors." They are exceptionally smart, capable, tough, and daring. At the same time, they were strangers to personal feelings, their own and other people's. Each of these women suffered from symptoms of severe depression, felt betrayed by the men, and were surprised at their own naïveté and miscalculations. Thus far, I have not had the opportunity to work with the Chinese men in comparable situations.

The professional encounters I have had so far with the new wave of immigrants from China, I am sure, are just the beginning of a much larger picture. These and others similar to them are the individuals who form the tapestry of war and peace, reflecting a global condition. They try to adapt to American life with memories of China of the past fifty years, as did the Chinese laborers of the last century with their particular memories. I work with them as immigrant parents of this new cycle as I work with the children of immigrant parents of the previous cycle. The waves in the sea of life will be forever rolling. They are the same waves and they are different waves. When I walk in areas of San Francisco where Asian residents dominate, I see and hear monolingual toddlers on the sidewalks, running and laughing. I see them as future American-educated, contributing members of this energetic fast-forward country. A few of them may even become psychologists. I smile.

References

Birrell, Anne (1993). *Chinese Mythology, An Introduction.* The Johns Hopkins, University Press.

Buss, David M., Abbot, Max, Angleitner, Alois, Asherian, Armen, Biaggio, Angela, Blanco-Villasenor, Angel, Bruchon-Schweitzer, M., Hai-Yuan Ch'U, Czapinski, Janusz, DeRaad, Boele, et al. (1990). "International Preferences in Selecting Mates." *Journal of Cross-Cultural Psychology, 21*(1): 5-47.

Doi, Takeo (1981). *The Anatomy of Dependence,* Second Edition. Kodanska International Ltd.

Eckholm, Erik (1998). "A Spectacular Tale in Its Mythic Home." *The New York Times,* September 1, p. B1.

Editorial (1997). *Asian Week,* October 24, p. 4.

Fairbank, John King (1992). *China, a New History.* Boston, MA: Harvard University Press, pp. 187-254.

Fei Xiaotong (1979a). "America Revisited," in R.D. Arkush and L.O. Lee (Eds.), *Land Without Ghosts.* Berkeley and Los Angeles, CA: University of California Press.

Fei Xiaotong (1979b). "The Shallowness of Cultural Tradition," in R.D. Arkush and L.O. Lee (Eds.), *Land Without Ghosts.* Berkeley and Los Angeles, CA: University of California Press.

Hall, Edward T. (1983). *Dance of Life.* New York: Doubleday.

Hong, Peter Y. (1998). "The Changing Face of Higher Education." *The Los Angeles Times,* July 14, p. 1.

Hsu, Francis L.K. (1971). "Homeostasis and Jen: Conceptual Tools for Advancing Psychological Anthropology." *American Anthropologist, 73*(1): 23-44.

Hsu, Francis L.K. (1981). *Americans and Chinese: Passage to Difference,* Third Edition. Honolulu, HI: The University Press of Hawaii.

Hune, Shirley and Chan, Keyan (1997). "All Things Being Equal." *Asian Week,* September 5, p. 11.

Johnson, Frank (1985). "Western Perspectives on Self," in A. Marsella, G. De Vos, and F. Hsu (Eds.), *Culture and Self* (pp. 89-138). New York and London: Tavilstock Publication.

Labi, Nadya (1998). "Nagano 1998." *Time,* March 2, pp. 67-68.

Lau, M.P. (1995). "Sex and Civilization in Modern China." *Transcultural Psychiatric Research Review, 17*(2): 137-156.

Lee, Bill Lann (1997). "A Promise to Uphold American Values." *Asian Week,* October 30, p. 9.

Lee Ye-yuan (1994). "A View of Chinese Character from Observing Her Ceremonies," in Y.Y. Lee and K.O. Yang (Eds.), *Chinese Character* (pp. 181-206) (in Chinese). Taiwan: Qui Guan Publications.

Liang Qichao (1903). "The Power and Threat of America," in R.D. Arkush and L.O. Lee (Eds.), *Land Without Ghosts.* Berkeley and Los Angeles, CA: University of California Press.

Locke, Gary (1997). "Progress and Political Power." *Asian Week,* August 22, p. 7.

Maynard, Isabelle (1996). *China Dreams: Growing Up Jewish in Tientsin.* University of Iowa Press.

Nee, Victor G. and Brett De Bary Nee (1972). *Longtime Californ': A Documentary Study of an American Chinatown.* New York: Random House.

New Continent (1997). "News from China." *New Continent,* April, p. 2.

Panesar, Randip P. (1998). "What It Takes to Be Mr. Asian." *Asian Week,* August 20, p. 13.

Qian Ning (1996). *Studying in U.S.A.* (in Chinese). Jiang Shu, China: Jiang Shu Weniji Publications.

The Repeal and Its Legacy (1993). A conference sponsored by the Chinese Historical Society of America and Asian American Studies of San Francisco State University. November 12-14, San Francisco, California.

Rosenblatt, Roger (1998). "Decent Exposure." *Time,* April 27, p. 86.

Said, Edward W. (1993). *Culture and Imperialism.* New York: Alfred A. Knopf.

Schneiter, Fred (1992). *Getting Along with the Chinese, for Fun and Profit.* Hong Kong: Asia 2000 Ltd., Hong Kong.

Stross, Randall E. (1990). *Bulls in the China Shop.* Honolulu, HI: University of Hawaii Press.

Sun Tzu (1988). *The Art of Strategy* (translated by R.L. Wing). New York: Doubleday.

Tung, May (1991). "Insight-Oriented Psychotherapy and the Chinese Patient." *American Journal of Orthopsychiatry, 61*(2): 186-194.

Tung, May (1994). "Symbolic Meanings of the Body in Chinese Culture and 'Somatization'." *Culture, Medicine, and Psychiatry, 18*(4): 483-492.

Yang, Mayfair M.H. (1994). *Gifts, Favors and Banquets: The Art of Social Relationships in China.* Ithaca, NY: Cornell University Press.

Yip, Alethea (1997a). "Symphony Conductor." *Asian Week,* May 30, p. 5.

Yip, Alethea (1997b). "Hate Crime Recorder." *Asian Week,* July 11, p. 9.

Yuan K'o and Chan Ming (1985). *A Source Book of Chinese Mythology Texts* (in Chinese). Chengdu, China: Sichuan Institute of Social Science.

Yung, Judy (1995). *Unbound Feet: A Social History of Chinese Women in San Francisco.* Berkeley and Los Angeles, CA: University of California Press.

Zhao Shiqing, Qu Guang, Peng Zhenglong, and Peng Tiensen (1994). "The Sex Ratio of Suicide Rates in China." *Crisis, 15*(1): 44-48.

Index

Adoption, Chinese girls, 51-52
American culture
    Doi's view of, 57
    Fei's view of, 58
"An" (peace), 6
Ancestor worship, and conflict, 29
Anger, in Chinese families, 68-69
Apartment-building neighbors, 20
The Art of Strategy (Sun Tzu), 50
Assertiveness, 15
Attraction, mutual, 17-18

Behavior, learned, 2
Birrell, Anne, 54
"Birth oracle," 8
Boldness, as American characteristic, 58
Boundary
    in dwellings, 19-22
    overlapping, 11
    personal, 12
Brazelton, T. Berry, 20
Buss, David, 17

Chan, Keyan, 28, 54
Ch'an Buddhism (Zen), 88
"The Changing Face of Higher
    Education" (Hong), 84
Chastity, 17
Chiku (to eat bitterness), 100
Children/youth
    T. Berry Brazelton on, 20
    in Chinese culture, 10
    conflict, with parents, 28-32
    and discrimination, 26-27, 32

Children/youth *(continued)*
    and family funerals, complaints, 29
    and language barriers,
        generational, 28
    as overseas students, 25-26
    and role reversal, generational, 29
    and socialization, 41-42
    and stereotypes, 32-33
    view of parents, 30
China, and integration, 90-97
*China Dreams: Growing Up Jewish
    in Tientsin* (Maynard), 56
Chinese American
    emotional awareness, 76-79
    family of origin, 8-10. *See also*
        Family, Chinese
    pioneers, 25-27
    second generation, 83-85. *See also*
        Integration
    self-identity, 10-16, 24-37
Chinese Central Television, 15
Chinese culture
    and children. *See* Children/youth
    family in. *See* Family, Chinese
    and gender differentiation
        men and, 47-50
        women and, 50-54
    integration of
        in America, 83-90
        in China, 90-97
    and linguistics, 72-76
    name, 6-10
    self in, 10-16
Chinese Exclusion Act of 1882, 27
Chinese New Year's parade, San
    Francisco, 88
Clarification, and emotion, 77

Heart, and Chinese language, 69-70
Homeland, desire for, 94-97
Homosexuality, 16
Hong, Peter Y., 84
Hsu, Apo, 68
Hsu, Francis L. K., 12, 24, 41
Human rights, 13-15
Hune, Shirley, 28
Hutong (cluster of homes), 19

Idioms, body-rooted, 69-72
Immigrants, new cycle of, 99-103.
    See also Chinese American
Individualism, dwellings and, 20-21
Inferiority, internalized, 37-38
    in China, 54-59
    and cultural differences, 41-47
        and men, 47-50
        and women, 50-54
    and integration, 81-83
Integration, 85-90
    in China, 90-97
    and inferiority, 81-83
    of second-generation Chinese
        Americans, 83-85
Intercultural comparisons, 12
Interdependency, Chinese, 13
    walls and, 20-21
Intergenerational conflict, 21
"International Preferences in
        Selecting Mates" (Buss), 17
Interpretation, emotion and, 79
Interracial couple, 11, 32
Invisibility, sense of, 1
Inwardness, Chinese tendency for,
    12-13

Jiang Zemin, 93
Jiu wenhua (wine culture), 48
Johnson, Frank, 12
Journalists, Chinese as, 88
The Joy Luck Club (movie), 88

Kailang zhishuai (straightforward
    and open), 72
Kao (to lean on), 7
Kurosawa, Akira, 45
Kwan, Michelle, 12-13, 25, 83-84

Labi, Nadya, 12, 13
Language barrier, generational, 28-29
Lau, M. P., 52
Lee, Bill Lann, 85
Lee Ye-yuan, 54
Levaco, Ron, 56
Li Bai (poet), 73
Liability, Asianness as a, 40
Liang Qichao, 14
Linguistics, cultural, 72-76
Liu xuesheng (overseas student), 25-26
Locke, Gary, 40
Love, and cultural linguistics, 74

"Made by Chinese" (label), 87
Majie (street scolding), 78-79
Manipulation, 65-66
Marriage
    of daughter, after death of, 53-54
    dissolution of, and psychotherapy,
        102
    partner, choosing a, 17-19
    self in, 16-19
Martial arts, 88
Masculinity, Chinese, 48-49
Maynard, Isabelle, 56
Men
    and gender differentiation, 47-50
    and marital partner, choosing a,
        17-18
Migration, 31-32
Ming (fate or destiny), 66
Minghun (wedding between a ghost
        and a man), 53
Mirrors, 23-24
    and American reflections, 32-33
    and cultural/racial distances, 33-37
    and familial input, 28-32
    and positive image, 90-97

Order Your Own Copy of
This Important Book for Your Personal Library!

CHINESE AMERICANS AND THEIR IMMIGRANT PARENTS
Conflict, Identity, and Values

_____ in hardbound at $39.95 (ISBN: 0-7890-1055-0)

_____ in softbound at $22.95 (ISBN: 0-7890-1056-9)

COST OF BOOKS_____

OUTSIDE USA/CANADA/
MEXICO: ADD 20%_____

POSTAGE & HANDLING_____
*(US: $3.00 for first book & $1.25
for each additional book)
Outside US: $4.75 for first book
& $1.75 for each additional book)*

SUBTOTAL_____

IN CANADA: ADD 7% GST_____

STATE TAX_____
*(NY, OH & MN residents, please
add appropriate local sales tax)*

FINAL TOTAL_____
*(If paying in Canadian funds,
convert using the current
exchange rate. UNESCO
coupons welcome.)*

☐ **BILL ME LATER:** ($5 service charge will be added)
(Bill-me option is good on US/Canada/Mexico orders only;
not good to jobbers, wholesalers, or subscription agencies.)

☐ Check here if billing address is different from
shipping address and attach purchase order and
billing address information.

Signature_____

☐ **PAYMENT ENCLOSED: $**_____

☐ **PLEASE CHARGE TO MY CREDIT CARD.**

☐ Visa   ☐ MasterCard   ☐ AmEx   ☐ Discover
☐ Diner's Club

Account #_____

Exp. Date_____

Signature_____

Prices in US dollars and subject to change without notice.

NAME _____

INSTITUTION _____

ADDRESS _____

CITY _____

STATE/ZIP _____

COUNTRY _____ COUNTY (NY residents only) _____

TEL _____ FAX _____

E-MAIL_____
May we use your e-mail address for confirmations and other types of information? ☐ Yes   ☐ No

Order From Your Local Bookstore or Directly From
The Haworth Press, Inc.
10 Alice Street, Binghamton, New York 13904-1580 • USA
TELEPHONE: 1-800-HAWORTH (1-800-429-6784) / Outside US/Canada: (607) 722-5857
FAX: 1-800-895-0582 / Outside US/Canada: (607) 772-6362
E-mail: getinfo@haworthpressinc.com
PLEASE PHOTOCOPY THIS FORM FOR YOUR PERSONAL USE.

BOF96